SHERLOCK HOLMES

ESCAPE ROOM PUZZLES

Portable Press
An imprint of Printers Row Publishing Group
9717 Pacific Heights Blvd, San Diego, CA 92121
www.portablepress.com • mail@portablepress.com

Portable Press
Publisher: Peter Norton • Associate Publisher: Ana Parker
Editor: Dan Mansfield
Acquisitions Editor: Kathryn Chipinka Dalby

Welbeck Publishing Group
Project Editor: Chris Mitchell
Project Designers: Luke Griffin and Martin Stiff
Production: Marion Storz

ISBN: 978-1-64517-742-5

Cover images: (pocket watch) Steve Allen/Shutterstock; (lock mechanism) donatas1205/Shutterstock; (map) Patrick Guenette/Alamy Stock Photo; (key and keyhole) Chones/Shutterstock; (frames) Roberto Castillo/Shutterstock; (decorative lines) blue pencil/Shutterstock

Printed in Dubai

25 24 23 22 21   1 2 3 4 5

SHERLOCK HOLMES

ESCAPE ROOM PUZZLES

SOLVE THE INTERACTIVE MYSTERIES TO HELP SHERLOCK OUTWIT HIS MOST DANGEROUS ENEMY

JAMES HAMER-MORTON
CREATOR OF DEADLOCKED ESCAPE ROOMS

PORTABLE
PRESS
San Diego, California

CONTENTS

Introduction 6

About the Author 8

Prologue 10

CHAPTER 1
221B Baker Street 16

CHAPTER 2
The Train to Cookham 34

CHAPTER 3
Homestead Mansion 54

CHAPTER 4
The Mind Palace 74

CHAPTER 5
The Operating Room 88

CHAPTER 6

The Church 104

CHAPTER 7

Scotland Yard 122

CHAPTER 8

The Cells 136

CHAPTER 9

The Circus 152

CHAPTER 10

The Theater 166

Difficult Hints 182

Medium Hints 186

Easy Hints 192

Solutions 198

INTRODUCTION

This book is probably different than any other puzzle book you've encountered—unless you've read the previous *Escape Room Puzzles* book.

Most puzzle books are orderly affairs, with regular structuring, clearly defined problems, and compact—if difficult—challenges. In other words, they are safe. This is a different beast. To get anywhere with *Sherlock Holmes Escape Room Puzzles,* you need to approach the book one section at a time.

Some chapters have more than one section, and each one is a puzzle made up of interlocking pieces. Some sections hinge on knowledge you acquired earlier on, while others are entirely self-contained. To help Dr. John Watson, Holmes's closest ally, through the trials inside this book, you'll often need to think outside the box.

The way to approach a section is to read it through, letting Watson show you the things he considers to be of importance. You'll know when you come to the end of the section, because he'll always make it clear that he needs to come up with an answer before he can proceed. Do not read on—the answer may be revealed on the next page.

Once you've read over the section, go back and look at it again. On this second pass, you'll know what it is you need to end up with—whether it's a word, a number of so many digits, or a certain pattern. The puzzles you have to solve in each section will stand out, but exactly how to combine them, or what order to start in, may be less obvious.

I knew I could proceed.

The text of the book will always guide you, but Watson's hand may be subtle in places. It may be as clear as seeing that one puzzle gives you a set of numbers as an answer, and another needs a set of numbers to

use as a starting point. Generally, everything you solve will lead on to something else that you can use, but there may be points where all factors of a section may provide you with information toward your final goal, solvable only through logical thinking.

So, each section is at the same time a set of puzzles, a collection of hints, and a carefully interlocking jigsaw.

As for hints, each chapter gives you three tiers—hard, medium, and easy—available at the end of the book. The hard hints are there to give you some inspiration on how to approach each separate puzzle. Maybe just knowing what to solve next will give you all you need, because the hints are provided in the order that you'll need them. The medium hints should help if you're stuck, and the easy hints are there for when you're baffled. They will signpost the way forward, although no puzzle in this book is truly easy, even with the hints. Take your time. Don't expect to sail through the book. Take breaks. Come back later. Give it the time to properly understand each part and you'll have far more satisfaction.

One final note. Some puzzles require physical manipulation to solve. When you see scissors and dotted lines, you'll probably need to cut things out and turn them into two- or three-dimensional shapes. Some of these may be needed later in the book, so keep everything you have cut out until you complete it. If you don't want to damage the book, these pages can be photocopied, and we have also provided a PDF of the "destructible" pages, accessed from the following QR code for you to print at full quality.

GOOD LUCK.

About the Author and Acknowledgments

Escape rooms are now everywhere. Live rooms, online virtual escapes (which Deadlocked is known for going all-out on), and, of course, now in printed media. This is the second escape room puzzles book I have written. The first, a modern-day exploration of my real-life escape room company, and Deadlocked Rooms' fictional Wexell Corporation, was successful around the world, and despite the huge amount of work, I was honored to be asked to write another. We learned from the first book how challenging the book could be for the reader, and so we have tried to make the difficulty curve a lot more gradual in this one.

The intention was to capture the feel of a real escape room, with a gradual unraveling of a series of puzzles in each chapter, while honoring the format itself to try to write an exciting story around everything— something Deadlocked Rooms is passionate about.

While the fan inside me is jumping up and down at having a Sherlock Holmes book published, I could not have done it without the amazing team behind it, and I'd like to thank them specifically. Chris, my publisher—thanks for being a source of positivity, encouragement, and fun. The ridiculously talented design team, who took my awful scrawled drawings of puzzles and made them look great. Judi, my mother— thank you for always supporting me so much, and doing a chunk of the grunt work in this when I was asking for a list of names, hairstyles, and that ridiculous mice puzzle! And, of course, Charlie, my partner and Deadlocked co-owner—thank you for helping to come up with a lot of the best content and magic. Everything we do is better with each other.

If you've enjoyed this, please feel free to check out the rest of our games (online and not) at www.deadlockedrooms.com—thanks for playing!

The Game Is Afoot

221B

I knew from the moment I read the telegrams from Holmes that this was serious. Certainly, he was never shy of overdramatizing minor inconveniences, but in these messages the jumble of information that I was presented with was confused, and his normal tone was missing. Knowing Holmes as I did, I was aware that he often hid information meant only for me, in case of interception. This must have been the case now.

Removing my key from my jacket pocket, where I had prepared it for swift access, I slid it into the front door of 221B Baker Street and turned it, springing the door open in one swift maneuver. Upon entry, I was faced with an unusual sight. The stairs up to Holmes's door had been vandalized with unfamiliar drawings. Shapes ran across each stair. I sensed something was amiss here, so I quickly sketched out the patterns in my case notebook.

Running up the stairs, I was faced with Mrs. Hudson, Holmes's landlady, who seemed both bemused and angry about the defacement of her building.

"Mr. Watson," she began. *"Do you have any idea what is going on with Sherlock?"*

"Good afternoon, Mrs. Hudson. I do not. Did Holmes have anything to do with the stairs?"

"He was in a flurry, Mr. Watson. He wouldn't stop, however loudly I shouted at him. Then he rushed up here and locked himself in his room. He's been playing his violin ever since."

Something seemed odd about the sound of the eerie scraping of Holmes's violin. I had a hunch but needed to get into his study to confirm it. A small padlock-type device was attached to a small bolt secured to the wooden door.

"He'll have to pay for that, you know," exclaimed Mrs. Hudson.

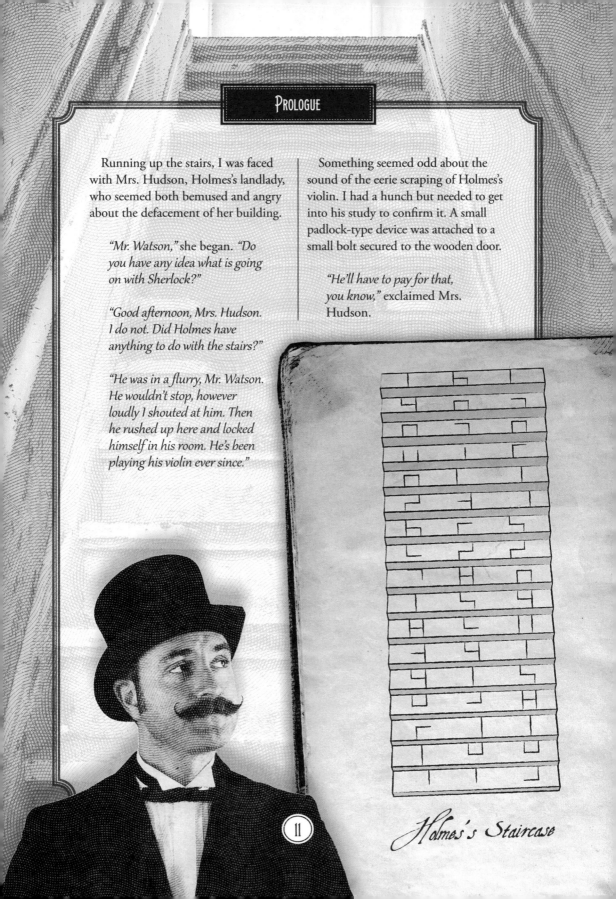

Holmes's Staircase

The lock was a simple metallic contraption that let the user open the device, if the tumblers are rotated into the correct position—but the code blocked even me, with my own key, from entering. Little did I know that solving this puzzle would be the simplest of all of the mysteries that I would be faced with in the next few days. Pondering the issue, I wondered if this had something to do with the series of telegrams that Holmes had sent to call me here.

Piecing some of them together, I realized three of the numbered telegrams formed a complete letter, concluding with his identifier: S. H. With the instructions given, I was able to discern how to approach the stairs that I had seen beforehand.

HINTS
Difficult, turn to page 182
Medium, turn to page 186
Easy, turn to page 192
For solutions, turn to page 198

Once I found my three-digit code, I knew I could proceed.

Date 06/20

TELEGRAM (2)
Date 20/94
Office Stamp

Dear Inspector,
Your latest investigations have amused me. The crime, obviously not, but your bungling of the confession, marked J. A.

TELEGRAM
Date 06/20/94
Office Stamp

Unfortunately, I need your experience presently at 221B Baker Street. Put these telegrams in order and use the identification numbers in this order in the next sentence.
(5)

ELEGRAM
Office Stamp

What he had done with this money was a tale for another day, but needless to say, Armitage wasn't the only man to have changed his name. — S. H.
(4)

TELEGRAM
Date 06/20/94
Office Stamp

Watson, This epistle reaches you, hopefully, in good spirits.
(1)

TELEGRAM
Date 06/20/94
Office S

The man in question was born James Armitage, hence the initials, and he had embezzled money from the bank where he worked.
(3)

TELEGRA
Date 06/20/94

Of seventeen from your entry, stack step ???, step ???, and step ??? from bottom to top to grant access — S. H.
(14)

The telegrams meant for me were numbered 1, 5, and 14. I took the lines drawn onto the steps and stacked them upon one another, forming some irregularly drawn, but clearly understandable, digits: 415. Spinning the lock into the correct formation, it sprang open. Despite the situation, I did chuckle when I tried the handle. Still locked. I would need my key after all. The lock was meant to delay—not prevent—especially because anyone with time to check all 1,000 combinations would be able to gain entry anyway.

However, even I was held out long enough for Holmes to complete his plans. I opened the door to find that my hunch was correct. The room was empty. The sound of the violin continued screeching through his gramophone.

CHAPTER ONE

221b BAKER STREET

The home of Sherlock Holmes. He was currently going through one of his erratic periods. His drug use was, as ever, a problem, albeit one that we had confronted on multiple occasions. On this occasion, however, it was affecting him differently. Ever since the death of Professor James Moriarty, Holmes had appeared unfocused and more worryingly paranoid than normal.

His scrambled telegrams suggested an escalation of this behavior. It seemed to me—someone who had the fortune to know his incredible mind well—as if he had lost something, or someone, valuable.

A short time ago, I had decided to return to live with Holmes—my own recent bereavement meant my state of mind aligned with his sense of loss. But merely a week before I was to move in,

Each chemical begins with a different letter, and the letter moves up and down in the alphabet depending on what is being done to it. The alphabet loops, so that the letter above Z is A.

Iron oxide—X, phosphorus—P, iodine—I, copper sulfate—S, mercury—M, copper chloride—C

When presented within the following items:
Straight-sided Beaker = + 5
Flask = - 8
Test Tube = + 2

When presented with the following modifiers:
When heated by a Bunsen burner = - 6
When water is dripped onto chemical = + 10
When another chemical (not water) is dripped onto chemical = + 5
When container is suspended horizontally = + 15

he had insisted I take some time away from him. At his request, strange as it was, I took a well-earned break at a lovely bed-and-breakfast that he had booked for me some distance from the center of London. Now, upon my return, I found that in my absence Holmes had most certainly been busy.

A complicated chemical experiment had been set up on a table near the door of his room. I cautiously stepped past, eyeing the strange notes that he had left beside it. Although he was not present, Holmes had left a Bunsen burner alight. This was reckless to say the least, and spoke volumes about his current state of mind. Before I turned it off, I quickly sketched the experiment in my notebook, thinking that I might need to show it to a particular chemist friend of mine later to ascertain what Holmes was trying to make.

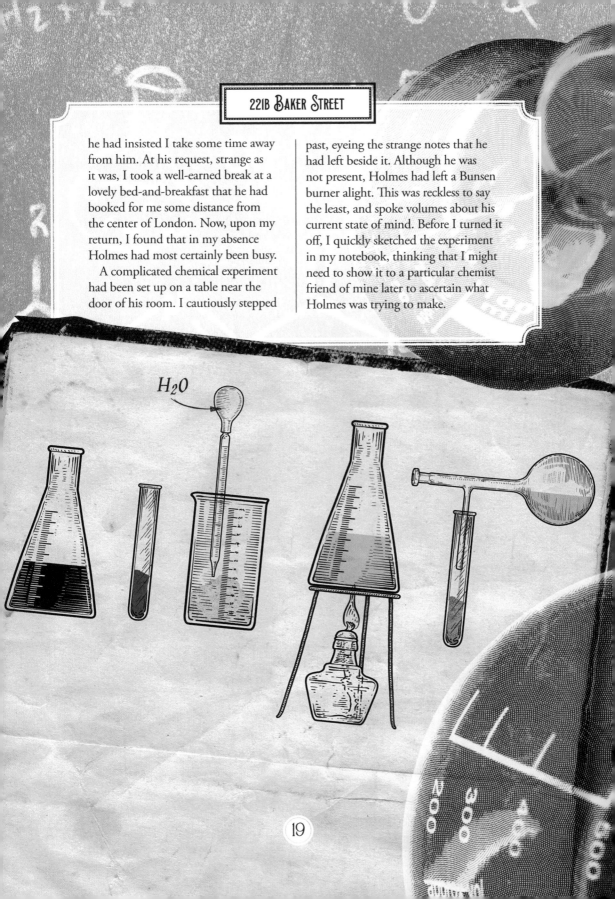

H_2O

I walked over to the gramophone and halted the concerto. The vinyl record that was playing felt unexpectedly different than normal on one side. A closer inspection suggested that Holmes had tampered with it; yes, the grooves and indents scratched into it were certainly unusual.

Even stranger was that he had used the item to falsify his presence at home. I wracked my brain to consider why he might have done so. Was he hiding from someone? And, at least until he had sent the cryptic telegrams, why was he hiding this information from me?

The answer was perhaps directly in front of me: I stared toward a cork board where Sherlock would often put up notes and articles about whatever he was working on—currently it seemed a French case had caught his interest. However, there was now a large empty calendar—one that I could not imagine Holmes purchasing—with today's date circled on it, June 20, 1894. Reaching out to examine it further, I noticed a letter hidden behind it meant for me. It appeared to have been written in a rush, because the handwriting was scribbled.

I scoured the room for any piece of information that might explain what my next move should be. Nothing immediately stood out. Next to his violin was the latest sheet music he had been reading from. One page was resting on the music stand and had been tampered with, as had the two pages scattered below.

Dear Watson,

I apologize for my absence and the deception surrounding your presence here. My injuries from the Falls have left me a shell of my former self. I have found myself questioning everything. The past, the Falls, even myself. When you cannot trust yourself, you may rely on only your closest friend. That, dear Watson, is you. There is a chance, of course, that someone else could stumble upon this, so I have hidden away what is necessary in the hope that you may deduce the solutions that will lead to me. You know how I work, because I often confide in you not only my results but also my methods. You are the most realistic expectation I have of success, and of my surviving the next few days.

Follow my trail. The first clue you notice in this room should leave you in no doubt as to what you must do next.

It may also be pertinent to you to know the places I have visited, and in which order. I have left a mark upon them with the information.

Carpe diem.

—S. H.

Red = phosphorus

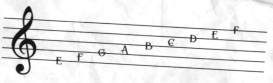

For #Sharp. add 5

Further investigation of the room led me to a wall of shelves covered in case files detailing Holmes's previous cases. The names of the clients were marked at the top of each, along with the date of when each case was solved. However, surprisingly for such a methodical person, Holmes had not arranged them in any obvious order, such as alphabetically or by date.

What's more, while I recognized some of the names as Holmes's larger cases—Baskerville and Hatherley—others were simple mysteries unraveled in front of the client without even leaving this room: for example Regan, Lewis, Cheriton. Cheriton was the most recent of his victories that I was aware of. A woman entered our premises under the guise of discovering who was responsible for her late husband's disappearance and probable death. She had presented to Holmes a threatening letter that her husband had been sent, along with an itinerary from her diary of where her husband was meant to be in the days leading up to his disappearance.

Mrs. Cheriton had insisted that her husband had not returned home on June 16, and wanted Holmes to help capture the man responsible. It took some time for me to deduce the obvious clue in the documentation that led to the solution.

Could you, dear reader, point out what was unusual about the case and identify the culprit?

Cheriton
6/94

Baskerville
10/89

Fletcher
11/88

Harris
5/87

Bond
1/89

O'Riley
2/90

Hansford
1/90

Regan
7/88

Ormstein
3/88

Painter
2/87

Openshaw
7/87

Mitchell
8/88

Morton
6/91

Peltzer
2/90

McCleod
4/91

Hatherley
5/89

Lewis
3/92

Hamer
5/91

Yellow = iron oxide

June 10[?]

Dear Mr. Cheriton,

Your meddling in my business has gone far enough.

If you undercut me with my suppliers once more, I will be forced to take action.

—A concerned citizen.

JUNE 1894

NOTES	SUN	MON	TUES	WED	THURS	FRI	SAT
_____						1	2
_____	3	4	5	6	7	8	9
_____	10	11	12	13 Meeting with bank	14	15	16 Supplier collection
_____	17	18	19	20	21	22	23
_____	24	25	26	27	28	29	30

As soon as he read the documents, Holmes began smiling quietly to himself. I knew that look. He had spied something that brought the whole case crashing down. It was then that I recognized the handwriting of the letter that she brought to him to be the same as that in her diary. The loop of her "p" was particularly damning. I proposed that it had been written by her, although not sent to the husband. He would have recognized the handwriting, of course, and acted upon it. Therefore, husband and wife must have been in cahoots.

Their motivation was probably due to the meeting with the bank the day before the purported threat had been created. A financial mishap, no doubt, stemming from their business—I surmised he was a storekeeper—becoming unprofitable through their attempts to undercut other local businesses. They were desperate to pay their suppliers on June 16. Attempting to reduce their competition by having Holmes pin a crime on their competitor was their misguided attempt at relieving their pressures. This truth was confirmed by the wife's reaction. It was hardly the most important of cases, however, so to place it among these others made it stand out.

Before I could look any further into it, a trembling voice came from the entrance of the room. Mrs. Hudson was peering inside.

"Dr. Watson, is there no sign of Mr. Holmes?"

"Unfortunately not, Mrs. Hudson. I fear he has acted rashly and caused further problems for us."

"Would you like a cup of tea to calm your nerves?"

"Thank you, but no. I must press on and discover what my friend's motivations were for this confusing amalgamation of items."

"I see he has been taking his photographs again."

"Yes, these are new. Not his best work; probably rushed, but certainly intriguing."

Mrs. Hudson turned to leave before turning back with some hesitancy.

"Dr. Watson, I must apologize."

"Whatever for?"

"When Mr. Holmes was not answering the door, and the racket was coming from the other side, I went outside to see if I could shout into an open window. Instead, I caught the attention of a passing policeman, and he, knowing Mr. Holmes by reputation, left to contact other officers about the disturbance."

"Mrs. Hudson, are you saying that we may have other guests soon?"

"I'm afraid so. I realize that this puts you in a difficult position, as you are trying to discover Mr. Holmes's reasons. The policemen will come in and disturb your evidence."

Copper sulfate = blue

"Then I will have to work quickly, Mrs. Hudson. Thank you for informing me."

She took her leave and I turned my attention to the new photographs in the room. They were of a number of storefronts from around the city.

Further inspection of them was probably necessary, but I had to continue searching. The difficulty of separating what was important and what was not was overridden by something in Holmes's original letter to me. *Carpe diem.* Why had he said that?

Might you, dear reader, have figured out where my next clue was hidden?

Seize the day. What day did he mean? I looked over at Holmes's letter and saw the calendar with today's date circled. It must have been important. I grasped at the page and looked on its reverse side. Sure enough, he had written more to me.

Also attached was a page with a key to translate Morse code. I had heard of the code before, and Holmes had chided me in the past for my inability to grasp it. It seems that he had remembered my lack of skill with the subject and had generously prevented me from the effort of needing to learn it myself. Now I had every clue I was going to get, I needed to figure out where the "final piece" he mentioned would be hidden.

Once I had this, I knew I could proceed.

Watson,

I am hoping that burying this in reams of other paperwork and investigatory intrigue will mean that only you will be able to find this in time. All you need to know to find the final piece of this puzzle, for now, is music, vinyl record, photos. but not necessarily dated in this order. This Morse code key may also be of use to you.

—S. H.

Mercury = silver

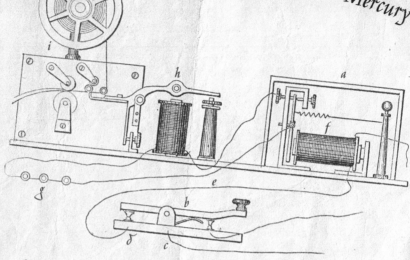

A	.−	N	−.	0	−−−−−
B	−...	O	−−−	1	.−−−−
C	−.−.	P	.−−.	2	..−−−
D	−..	Q	−−.−	3	...−−
E	.	R	.−.	4	....−
F	..−.	S	...	5	.....
G	−−.	T	−	6	−....
H	....	U	..−	7	−−...
I	..	V	...−	8	−−−..
J	.−−−	W	.−−	9	−−−−.
K	−.−	X	−..−		
L	.−..	Y	−.−−		
M	−−	Z	−−..		

HINTS
Difficult, turn to page 182
Medium, turn to page 186
Easy, turn to page 192
For solutions, turn to page 198

After translating the items around the room into names of the case files, and tracing out numbers using Holmes's filing system, I was able to determine a three-digit number, which I quickly noticed was the date on one of the case files. I plucked it out with some determination, only for a small slip of paper to fall from the back of it. It was a train ticket for this evening from London to Cookham, a small village in Berkshire county.

I wasted no time, and quickly packed a change of clothes into a suitcase before returning to take one final look around the room to see if there was anything I had missed. One painting, depicting a placid countryside scene, seemed like an odd piece for Holmes to have collected. It was new and readily portable; it already appeared to have been wrapped and prepared for transportation. I decided to take it with me in case Holmes needed it.

I donned my coat, swung the door closed, and locked it behind me. Standing in front of me was a familiar face: a dark-eyed fellow by the name of Inspector Lestrade.

"Dr. Watson, I am pleased to see you here."

"Inspector, it is a welcome surprise, of course, to see you. However, I must take my leave presently as I have a train to catch."

"Before you leave, Mrs. Hudson expressed concern about the whereabouts of Mr. Sherlock Holmes. I must ask, is this something for us to be concerned about?"

"Honestly, Inspector, I cannot be sure. Holmes has left instructions for me to follow, so I can only assume that he is acting freely and all is under control, but I will, of course, update you on anything I discover."

"Thank you, Doctor."

Lestrade bowed and took his leave. I followed swiftly and found a hansom cab to take me to the train station for my onward journey. A change of trains would be necessary in Maidenhead, but the timing would leave me plenty of leeway; reaching my first train was the challenge. Had Holmes planned to leave me no time, in order to make sure that I would have to be on top of my game to succeed at 221B Baker Street? Whatever his intentions, I just managed to catch the train.

Upon arrival, I took an opportunity to breathe the air outside London. It was a treat, lacking the heaviness of London's atmosphere. The sun was going down as I waited patiently for my train to Cookham to arrive and various other passengers found their connections. Eventually, I stood alone on the station platform. All was quiet until a small but well-maintained locomotive approached. As I confirmed the time, the conductor stepped off the train and shouted the names of stations. I listened for Cookham, and boarded as soon as I heard it mentioned. The door was locked behind me and, slowly, we pulled away.

CHAPTER TWO

THE TRAIN TO COOKHAM

I had in my possession a remarkable combination of unlikely items. A painting packaged by my friend Sherlock Holmes, a selection of clothing for which there was no point or purpose—because I did not know my ultimate purpose for traveling—and a ticket to a small town that I had no intention or desire to visit before Holmes forced me onto this train.

The passenger coach itself seemed well maintained, or perhaps new enough that bad maintenance had never reared its head. I had noticed a Pullman car, which would let me procure sustenance on this train. The pangs of hunger were beginning to hit me, so if I had the time, I might investigate it, but it was late enough in the evening that I did not expect more than a half-decent service.

Unusually, I saw early on that the coach in which I was placed, made up of three separate rooms, was empty of passengers beside myself. My ticket was for compartment three, and a quick glance as I walked past the others confirmed that I was alone. I took my seat and deposited my suitcase in the overhead storage area before my thoughts wandered to my ultimate purpose for being here. It would hopefully become clear when I arrived, yet I couldn't imagine how. Perhaps a driver would be waiting for me? Could Holmes have sent someone, or even himself, to intercept me?

A loud hammering on the door just outside my room interrupted my reverie. I questioned whether this was all part of my friend's plan and leaped to my feet to investigate the cacophony. Alas, it was just a ticket collector, garbed in a large overcoat and circular hat, rapping at the window. He was seemingly unable to open the door from the other coach. I tried it myself but couldn't see a way of releasing the lock without the key that had obviously caused this mess.

"Open the door!" he shouted through the thin glass.

"I'm afraid I do not have a key to do so," I admitted.

"So how did you lock it?"

"I did no such thing."

"I need to check your ticket."

I raised my ticket to the glass to a confused nod from the collector.

". . . and if you see a way of opening this, then that'd be useful."

"Of course. I am sorry."

He slunk away, while I wandered back, apologizing for something that was not my fault at all, as far as I knew. Out of interest, I hurried over to the other side of the carriage and tried that door.

It was locked, too. How unusual. I returned to my seat and was pondering what could have caused this situation, when we pulled into a station—not my destination. I watched from the window as the ticket collector took up a small limping jog to reach the entrance to my coach. He tried the door there, and that too would not open. He came to my window.

"If you've done this, you're going to be in big trouble."

"I can assure you I had n-nothing to d-do with this," I stuttered.

Perhaps the maintenance of the coach was not as good as I had previously assumed.

"Where are you going?"

"Cookham."

"All right, well, just sit tight for now, and I'll speak to the driver. We'll figure something out by then."

He rushed back inside, the conductor blew a whistle, and the train started moving again. A feeling of ominous realization rolled down my spine. Of course. Sherlock, or someone involved in this case, had set this up. There must be something I should do while inside. I jumped to my feet as the train pulled away. My time was running out, and I needed to solve this puzzle before my stop.

I investigated the doors leading to other coaches. The one the ticket collector had tried to open previously had a map of the train line on it. The stations, however, were bizarrely obscured, so I could not tell how far it was to my stop. I saw the scale in one corner of it, which informed me how many miles were in each inch of the drawing.

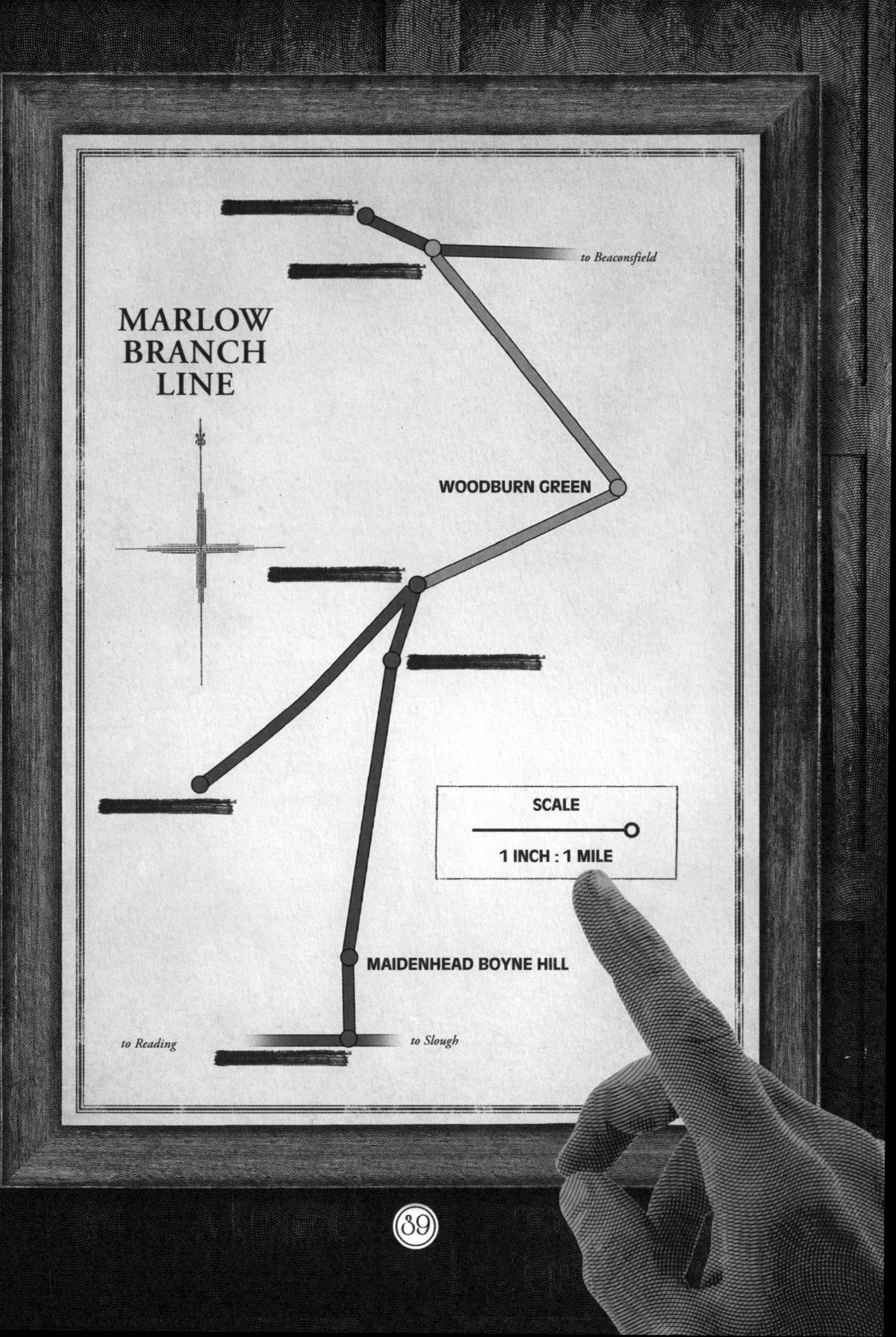

MARLOW
BRANCH
LINE

to Beaconsfield

WOODBURN GREEN

SCALE

1 INCH : 1 MILE

MAIDENHEAD BOYNE HILL

to Reading   *to Slough*

On the door on the opposite side was a sign indicating that the restaurant car was in that direction. My stomach growled as I spied a menu with a plethora of options. The items were very specific about what ingredients went into them, but perhaps it was to make sure that anyone with allergies would not be caught amiss.

Train Store Inventory (prejourney):

Each list item is counted in terms of servings needed to create a meal.

Baking Powder—32
Beef—25
Butter—28
Chicken—19
Chocolate—32
Corn—10
Flour—10
Garlic—9
Green bell pepper—22
Milk—10

Oats—29
Onion—34
Paprika—16
Pork—5
Salt—47
Sugar—33
Tomato—14
Vinegar—32
Water—15

```
MESSAGE FROM MANAGEMENT:
------------------------
Dear Mr. Jones, I am concerned about the stores we have
of each item to run a fully capable dining coach.
    I am particularly intrigued by the number of the
following ingredients left after staff meals have been
made.
    Onion, Tomato, Milk
Beef, Green Bell Pepper, Salt, Butter, Chocolate.
    These numbers mean something to me, even if they do not
to you. We are trying to provide an Al service here.

Samuel Hardington
```

RESTAURANT MENU

Each item contains one serving of each ingredient, for reference

HAMBURGER
Ingredients: Beef, Onion, Green Bell Pepper, Water, Vinegar, Paprika, Salt.

GOULASH
Ingredients: Beef, Onion, Garlic, Water, Salt, Butter, Sugar, Flour

CHICKEN PIE
Ingredients: Chicken, Onion, Green Bell Pepper, Salt, Tomato, Water, Corn

BEEF PIE
Ingredients: Like Chicken pie, but with Beef replacing Chicken and no Bell Pepper

PORK RIBS
Ingredients: Pork, Onion, Tomato, Water, Vinegar, Salt, Paprika

FUDGE DESSERT
Ingredients: Sugar, Butter, Salt, Milk, Chocolate

MOTHER'S COOKIES
Ingredients: Flour, Oats, Baking Powder, Salt, Chocolate, Butter, Sugar

Staff Order

For any train with a dining coach, the staff tend to order exactly the same thing, depending on their job.

I have noticed that Drivers will always pick Goulash as a main and Mother's Cookies as a dessert.

Each Ticket Inspector will choose a Hamburger followed by a Fudge Dessert.

Waiters only pick a main dish: Pork Ribs.

Any Train Guard will go for just the Chicken Pie.

Haulers will take a serving of Beef Pie and Mother's Cookies.

Chefs are the only staff member that varies, selecting the most popular main dish and dessert from the other staff picks.

As I passed the first of the three compartments on my way back to my own, I noticed something unusual. Despite there being no other passengers around me, a collection of multicolor suitcases sat in the rack over the seats. Looking closer, I saw that some of the suitcases had an identification tag on them, with the name of the owner or their intended traveling route, but other tags lay scattered haphazardly beneath them.

It took me just a short time to deduce two things about these six suitcases that were unusual. One confirmed that they had been left for me, and the other indicated that my previous assumptions were wrong.

Could you, dear reader, surmise either or both of my breakthroughs before you proceed?

Owen
Paris–Berlin

Willis

Abbey

Smith

Marlow to
Bourne End
2 miles

Nicholson

Trevor

While I lacked knowledge regarding every stop on this train's route, Paris and Berlin were clearly not possible stops! What was that suitcase doing here, unless it—and probably the rest of them—had been placed here for some specific reason?

The second clue was the names of the passengers. The first letter of each spelled out "W a t s o n." All of the suitcases were on this train for my benefit. Had Holmes managed to plant them himself, or did he goad another passenger into creating this selection? Surely getting them all on board had taken more than just one individual working in secrecy.

I took a step backward to get an overview of the suitcases. I moved too far, in fact, and struck the seats behind, jolting me down onto their surprisingly firm surface. From this angle, however, I could see a small cream rectangle poking out from underneath one of the cases. I reached out and pulled a small envelope from the hidden crevice. It had my name upon its front, clearly in Holmes's handwriting. I tore it open, eager to find a clue within.

Dear Watson, my reliable companion,

Your mind must be racing with questions and confusion over my disappearance. Indeed, I am lucky enough to have had the foresight to prepare for my unfortunate circumstances. I cannot answer the obvious question of who is responsible without altering my only form of restitution. Also, responsibility is not as simple as the identity of the man that forced me from my home. I promise to you, dear Watson, that if you can reach me before it is too late, all will become clear. Until then, it is important you know that you are on the right track, if you will excuse the pun, and to know the following:

- High Wycombe to Marlow is a shorter journey than Maidenhead to High Wycombe.
- The smallest case is traveling 6 miles.
- Abbey has a larger case than Willis.
- The largest case travels 7 miles.
- The black case travels between Cookham and Loudwater.
- Abbey is traveling between High Wycombe and Loudwater.
- Nicholson is traveling 2 miles.
- The longest route is 545 miles, between Paris and Berlin.
- It is 4 miles from Cookham to Loudwater.
- The shortest route is ½ mile.
- Willis is traveling farther than Trevor.

Now, it is important that you get started, and I have left you a simple tool that may prove to be useful to you on your journey. It is situated in the single item of luggage that you can open, in a hidden inset on the underside of the top.

I hope that I will see you soon, Watson.

—S. H.

One of the suitcases had to be unlocked. I quickly made for them and tried one after the other. Much to my chagrin, none were unlocked. I rechecked the letter; Holmes had implied that I would be able to open one. He did not, however, tell me that I would be able to do so immediately. Perhaps he had hidden a key elsewhere? I decided to move on for now, but I did not understand where I was to begin.

Holmes had stumped me already. What if I was to be of no help in rescuing him from his adversary? I returned to my own compartment, dejected, until I saw something in there that I realized I should have understood immediately from Holmes's letter.

Can you, dear reader, work out what I had neglected to consider earlier before you proceed?

Name	Route	Distance	Color of Suitcase	Suitcase Size (1-6)
Abbey				
Nicholson				
Owen				
Smith				
Trevor				
Willis				

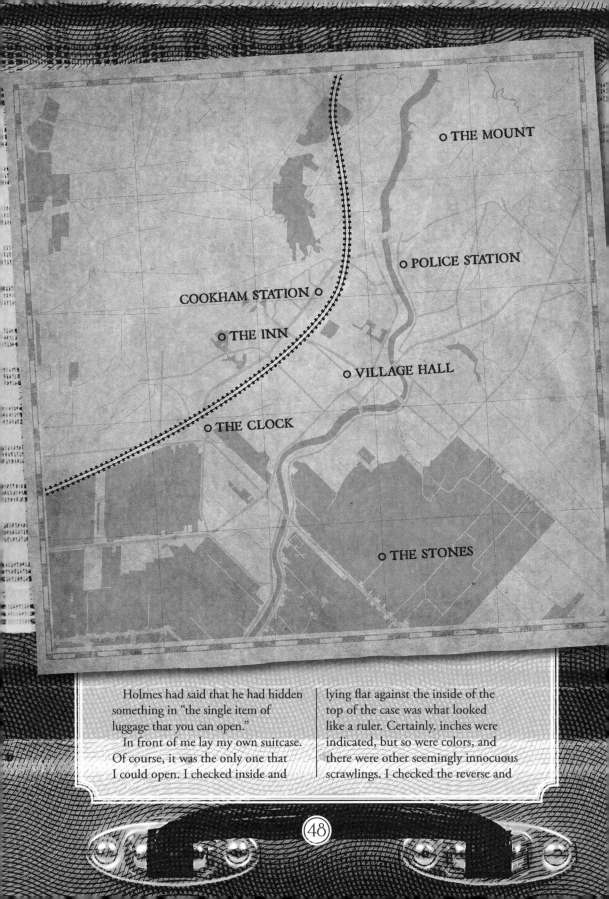

Holmes had said that he had hidden something in "the single item of luggage that you can open."

In front of me lay my own suitcase. Of course, it was the only one that I could open. I checked inside and lying flat against the inside of the top of the case was what looked like a ruler. Certainly, inches were indicated, but so were colors, and there were other seemingly innocuous scrawlings. I checked the reverse and

it had further information for me. The entire alphabet was labeled along one of the edges, and I quickly realized that it had more uses than I could initially surmise. In the center was an interesting symbol. It appeared to read SH—Sherlock Holmes—yet when spun upside down it read the same thing. It was a unique design, and one that I knew he had put there for a reason. Beside the ruler lay a small map of Cookham. A few names were noted there; perhaps one of them would be my final destination?

I still had one more room to investigate, the central room of the coach. I took a deep breath and turned the handle on the door. It did not budge. I could only assume that it was locked, but because of its glass panel I could see what was inside. A small wooden train had been set up, its track running around the floor. I don't know how I had missed it before, when I glanced in, but then again I had only been checking to see if it was occupied or not.

"I TOOK A DEEP BREATH AND TURNED THE HANDLE ON THE DOOR."

A	B	C
D	E	F
G	H	I
J	K	L
M	N	O
P	Q	R
S	T	U
V	W	X
Y	Z	

A	**B**	**C**
D	**E**	**F**
G	**H**	**I**
J	**K**	**L**
M	**N**	**O**
P	**Q**	**R**
S	**T**	**U**
V	**W**	**X**
Y	**Z**	

S1

N2

E3

W4

Perhaps because the door was locked, I was not meant to be able to move the trains. The way it was set up must be important. I quickly sketched the various objects, and as I did so, I saw the corner of a sheet of paper emerging from underneath the door. I transcribed the information beneath my sketch and returned to my coach to study the results.

Taking account of all circumstances surrounding my own capture within this coach, and starting with Holmes's letter, I had to follow the clues. And before I arrived in Cookham, I needed to find the name of my destination there.

Once I had this, I knew I could proceed.

HINTS
Difficult, turn to page 182
Medium, turn to page 186
Easy, turn to page 192
For solutions, turn to page 200

Cookham to Loudwater (4 miles, 3 stops)

P P D P P D P P L G G G

P P

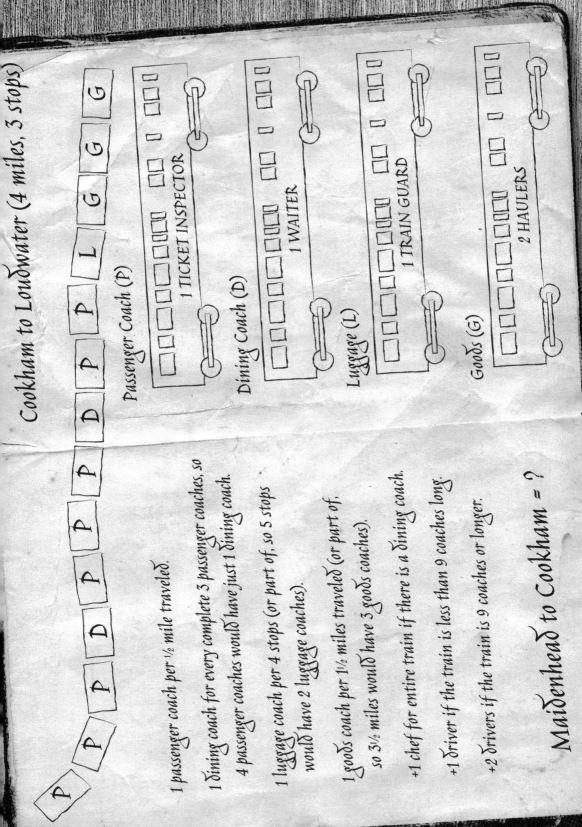

Passenger Coach (P)

1 TICKET INSPECTOR

Dining Coach (D)

1 WAITER

Luggage (L)

1 TRAIN GUARD

Goods (G)

2 HAULERS

1 passenger coach per ½ mile traveled.

1 dining coach for every complete 3 passenger coaches, so 4 passenger coaches would have just 1 dining coach.

1 luggage coach per 4 stops (or part of, so 5 stops would have 2 luggage coaches).

1 goods coach per 1½ miles traveled (or part of, so 3½ miles would have 3 goods coaches).

+1 chef for entire train if there is a dining coach.

+1 driver if the train is less than 9 coaches long.

+2 drivers if the train is 9 coaches or longer.

Maidenhead to Cookham = ?

I found two words. "The Mount." Cross-checking the words I had found against the map, I traced my fingers across the paper, which confirmed The Mount was a house in Cookham.

Something else was amiss. Underneath the name was a solid bulge in the paper. It seemed to be a small, rectangular, metallic-feeling shape. I pushed it to the edge of the paper, which ripped the side open. Out fell a key. Holmes had hidden a small key inside the map, and I knew instantly where to use it.

I picked up my suitcase, straightened my shirt, and strode to the coach door as it pulled into Cookham. The key slid effortlessly into the small hole on the door and released me from my vehicular prison. I took a deep breath and stepped onto the platform. Breathing out revealed the cold in the air, which made me instinctively shiver. I looked around and saw only the silhouette of the ticket collector rushing toward me. I held up the key, which he grabbed from me. I was expecting an accusatory stare, but instead he smiled and nodded. Had he been in on this all along?

The lights in the area were dim and stark. The mist of the countryside was sweeping into the station, and as the train pulled away, leaving me in silence, I could see a small outline of a child in the distance.

"You there, boy!" I shouted.

It was enough to cause him to flee into the distance. I pursued, in the hope that at least he would not be leading me into further peril. It was normally Holmes that had his Irregulars, but I thought it was worth a shot.

I emerged through the archway that the boy had run through to find a lone horse-drawn carriage in front of me. I approached the driver.

"Excuse me, my good sir?"

"Where are you going?" he questioned somewhat abrasively.

"To . . ." I paused. Was my destination itself the puzzle, or a code word to say to this gentleman? Or should I hold the information to myself?

"Spit it out, man," he insisted.

I decided to take a risk.

"The Mount."

"Mr. Watson, I assume?"

My secrets had already been well and truly spilled.

"Well, get in then," he continued.

I obliged, hoisting my own suitcase inside, thinking that perhaps his services did not extend to assistance with luggage. I planted myself on the more comfortable seats and turned my head to see a tiny face staring up at me. It must have been the boy I'd seen earlier.

"I'm Stanley," the boy announced.

"Good evening to you, young man. My name is Dr. John Watson."

"Are you a friend of the man?"

"Shut up, Stanley," the driver barked.

The journey continued in silence. Whatever young Stanley had accidentally revealed would be more pertinent to me than he knew.

We arrived at a humble house, in my opinion not befitting of the name it had been given. I stepped out and was met with the shadow of a woman in the doorway. I took my case and started approaching the path. I heard a sharp sound and my eyes darted down to see movement. A cage with chickens was in the yard, right beside me. I had grown used to the sounds of the city. Chickens were a welcome departure, yet I felt alone and vulnerable. By the time I looked back up, the door was closed.

"You're not going in there," the driver began. "Up that path."

He nodded toward the mist. A small isolated cobblestone path emerged from the darkness. I felt my jacket for some remuneration for the man's assistance.

"Don't worry about that, the ride is already paid for. You've got bigger problems ahead of you."

"Thank you, my good man," I replied, quivering at either the cold or the anxiety of the unknown ahead of me.

Not wanting to appear nervous, I marched along the path, as if it were

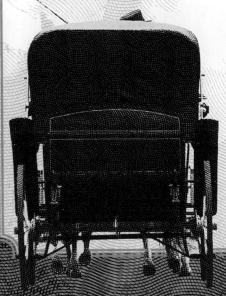

a normal occurrence to be in the middle of nowhere with little vision ahead, never mind knowledge of my route or my intentions. The path led downhill and my eyes acclimatized quickly as I moved farther toward what I assumed was The Mount.

After a hundred feet or so, I could make out a faint golden glow. I strode forward, feeling nothing but holding on to hope. My distance to the glow shortened, and as it did, more was revealed. It was a large mansion, candles illuminating the windows and a line of oil lamps showing me the route to the front door of what I now realized was my destination. I squinted in an attempt to see movement inside, so that I was prepared for what was to come. Nothing but flickering lighting within. I hoped that this would be the end of it, that the grand house contained all the answers I sought.

In fact, this was just the beginning of a new adventure, the details of which would be revealed only when I had completely explored the building. I was but at the entrance. A swift rapping on the thick black door was met with no response, so I was left with no choice but to breach the threshold and investigate the mysteries inside. I tried the door.

Unlocked.

I crept inside, ahead of me an enormous mansion to explore.

Well, there was no time like the present.

CHAPTER THREE
HOMESTEAD MANSION

The lavish entrance hall to the mansion sprawled out in front of me. Everywhere I looked, I noticed exquisite taste and expense. A large staircase in front of me led to another floor in the house; a corridor stretching underneath it would give me access to the rest of the first floor. Beside the stairs was a small table with a large sheet of paper prominently displayed on top of it. As eager as I was to investigate and explore, I felt it wise to announce my arrival, in case there was another presence in my vicinity.

"Excuse me, is anybody there?" I barked.

The silence that greeted me was punctured only by creaking floorboards and the wind outside. I could not tell if the two were linked or if another person was wandering the grand halls. I paused for another second or two, in case someone was coming to greet me, but no one emerged. I half expected a maid or butler, which would have been fitting given the appointments around me.

Cautiously, I moved over to the table and looked down. The sheet of paper was a map, which I assumed was of the mansion itself. On the bottom left was imprinted "Homestead Mansion." That, then, seemed to be the name of the building—a little more impressive than "The Mount." The map was split into a grid of squares, and I was standing precisely in the square marked "Start," just off the main entrance to the building.

A helpful compass on the other side of the map informed me of the direction the building was facing. I had a hunch that remembering this would assist me later on. There must be a reason to show the orientation of the building so explicitly.

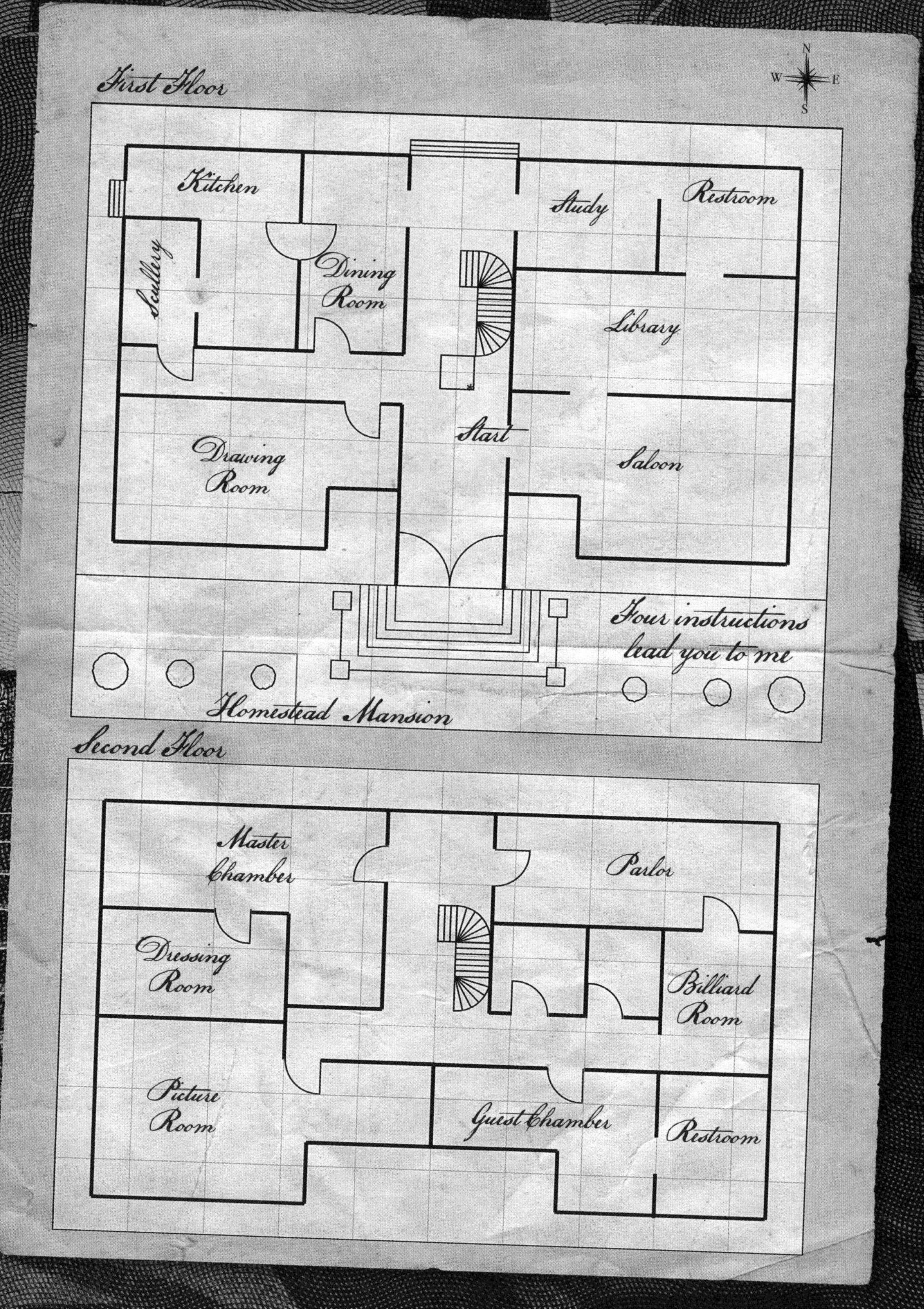

First Floor

Kitchen

Scullery

Dining Room

Study

Restroom

Library

Drawing Room

Start

Saloon

Four instructions lead you to me

Homestead Mansion

Second Floor

Master Chamber

Parlor

Dressing Room

Billiard Room

Picture Room

Guest Chamber

Restroom

Studying the map in more detail, I felt intrigued enough to walk the hall in order to investigate the rooms properly. At the bottom was written: "Four instructions lead you to me"— clearly an invitation to proceed, and confirmation that I had discovered what I was meant to. Although I was ignoring much social convention already, I felt it was a step too far to proceed inside with my hat on. Seeing a nearby hat stand, I removed it, leaving my suitcase alongside. A deep breath gave me the impetus to continue and, with newfound confidence adding a spring to my step, I marched down the corridor on the left toward my first port of call: the drawing room.

The doors in the building were thick and heavy and, at first, I assumed the door to my first room was locked. However, with a braver shove, it opened. The room that greeted me was lavish and stylish once again, with combinations of burgundy and gold flourishes: the curtains were burgundy, the furniture painted gold, decorated with burgundy cushions. I paused for a second to admire the unusual artwork, hung in the shape of what looked, perhaps fancifully, like another addition symbol. The center piece contained the word "MISSING" with the letters N E S W carved into the four edges. It was unusual enough that I felt that it had to be a clue of some kind.

Beside the carving was a large bookshelf with a collection that must have cost a pretty penny. Rare copies of unusual books suggested the owner was wealthy, although I did wonder if they were there more for show than for reading.

A table between the seats revealed the recent pastime of the mansion's inhabitants: a game of cards had been played, although I could not deduce the game in question from the setup. While the room was decadently furnished, there was little else that stood out to me and, given the encouragement of the map, I concluded that anything pertinent to my investigation would be more obvious than not. With many rooms to explore, I decided to move on.

As I left, directly opposite me I spied a door left ajar. I hesitated for a second but realized that I was too far in now to stop my search. It was the dining room.

The main feature of the room was a long oak table, but overall the room was more sparsely decorated than the last. The table had space for ten guests: four on each side and two heads of table. One of the chairs was noticeably grander than the others. A chest of drawers, no doubt containing cutlery, was locked with a key that I could not discover, despite a rigorous search. In one corner was a large cabinet display case that contained a collection of china plates of different patterns. I counted 30 plates and noted the immaculate display. It was clearly something of which the owner was proud.

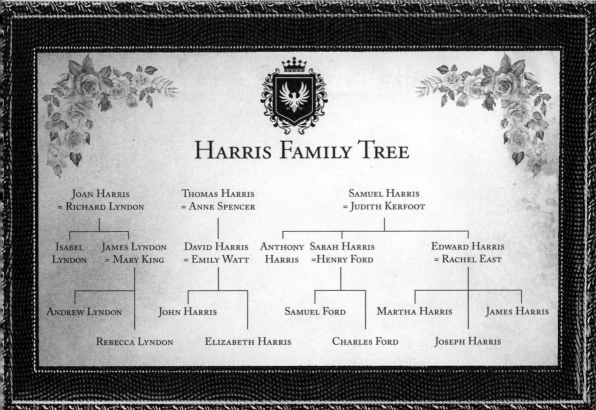

Harris Family Tree

Joan Harris = Richard Lyndon

- Isabel Lyndon
- James Lyndon = Mary King
  - Andrew Lyndon
  - Rebecca Lyndon

Thomas Harris = Anne Spencer

- David Harris = Emily Watt
  - John Harris
  - Elizabeth Harris

Samuel Harris = Judith Kerfoot

- Anthony Harris
- Sarah Harris = Henry Ford
  - Samuel Ford
  - Charles Ford
- Edward Harris = Rachel East
  - Martha Harris
  - Joseph Harris
  - James Harris

On the opposite wall was a prominent framed document showing what I assumed to be a recent family tree of the owners of the mansion. I looked at a few names, but nothing immediately stood out. Holmes was not on there—my first hunch rejected by this fact. I hesitated, before deciding I should not loiter when there was so much more to explore.

Another door from the dining room led into the kitchen. Any staff employed in the house may well have been in here, but, again, it was empty. A large series of tiled glass-fronted cabinets were hung over the top of a stove and coal ovens. Countertops for preparation were clean and well maintained, a sign of an efficient staff; however, the center table had a large number of kitchen utensils, pots, and pans upon it. It quickly became apparent that something was not right.

The cabinets had been completely emptied of their contents onto the table, which was itself divided up into a grid of squares. What's more, although I wasn't certain, I was sure there were too many items to fit into the available cabinet space. Upon further inspection, I saw that each of them had yellow lines of varying lengths marked onto them. What could they mean?

"I HAD NEVER SEEN A KITCHEN LEFT IN SUCH A STATE BEFORE."

A back door from this room opened to the scullery, a modest room containing staff uniforms and a large sink for cleaning. I found a staff rota that seemed unusually detailed and lengthy, with more staff than seemed necessary for a house of this size. Perhaps our lord of the manor enjoyed employing more workers than needed and spacing out their workload?

STAFF INFORMATION

Hours taken for each job

	Days of work	Gardening	Washing Clothes	Cooking	Dish washing	Cleaning House
John	Friday	4	1.5	2.5	0.5	2
Mary	Monday Friday Sunday	N/A	1	2	0.5	1
Leonard	Monday Wednesday Saturday	N/A	2	2.5	1	3
Shirley	Tuesday Wednesday Sunday	N/A	1.5	2	0.5	4
Anna	Tuesday Thursday Saturday	N/A	1	1.5	1	2.5

Each staff member can have multiple tasks in a day.

The master of the house is interested in only the total number of hours worked per day for all staff combined—I assume to be sure of adequate budgeting for staff.

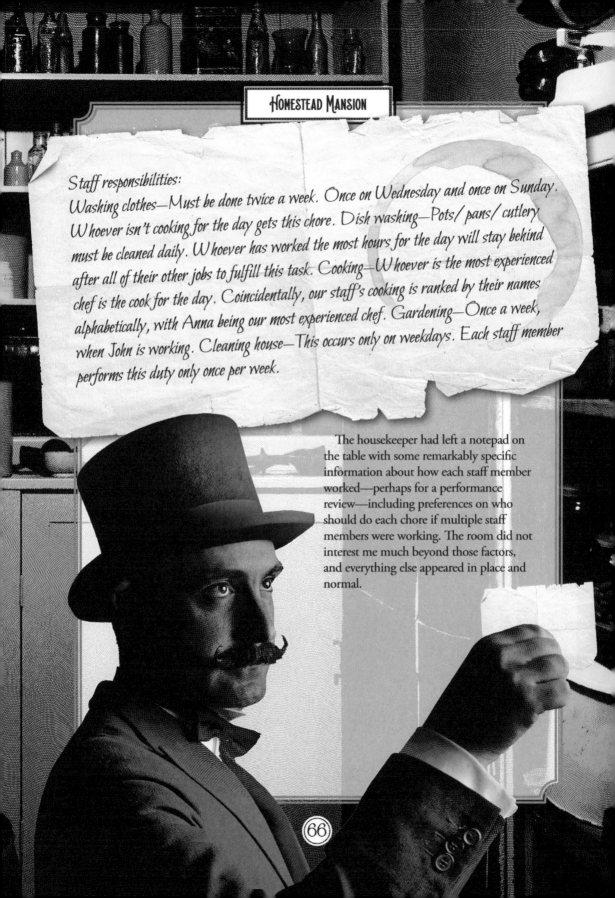

Staff responsibilities:

Washing clothes—Must be done twice a week. Once on Wednesday and once on Sunday. Whoever isn't cooking for the day gets this chore. Dish washing—Pots/pans/cutlery must be cleaned daily. Whoever has worked the most hours for the day will stay behind after all of their other jobs to fulfill this task. Cooking—Whoever is the most experienced chef is the cook for the day. Coincidentally, our staff's cooking is ranked by their names alphabetically, with Anna being our most experienced chef. Gardening—Once a week, when John is working. Cleaning house—This occurs only on weekdays. Each staff member performs this duty only once per week.

The housekeeper had left a notepad on the table with some remarkably specific information about how each staff member worked—perhaps for a performance review—including preferences on who should do each chore if multiple staff members were working. The room did not interest me much beyond those factors, and everything else appeared in place and normal.

I went out the other door, back into the main hallway. No other doors were unlocked on the first floor, persuading me to continue my search upstairs.

It felt more intrusive to be walking up the stairs of someone else's home without their knowledge. Halfway up, I saw a man's portrait on the wall, with his name and a quote underneath it: "My grandson is always welcome here—Thomas Harris." After considering the quote, I smiled. It was just possible that it was a simple coincidence, but the message behind the play on words surely indicated that I should be there.

Can you, dear reader, deduce what tickled me about what I had discovered?!!!

Thomas Harris's quotation stated that his grandson would "always be welcome here." Thinking back to the family tree, Thomas Harris had just one grandson, John Harris. His mother, however, was Emily Watt. In a way, that made him Watt's son: John Watson. Perhaps the spelling was not exactly right, but it made enough sense to me that it had to be deliberate. I would have to keep my wits about me if such linguistic acrobatics could be a viable solution.

At the top of the stairs to my left was the master bedchamber. Earlier I had merely been feeling intrusive. Entering this room increased my unease multiple times over, because etiquette decreed that it should be a private space. I decided to look elsewhere for now, leaving the room until I had no other options to investigate. However, almost everywhere else I was faced with locked doors. Whether the rooms within were unimportant, or I was meant to find a method of entry elsewhere, I did not know. The only exception was an unlocked door on the opposite side of the hallway from the bedchamber, allowing for access to the parlor.

Immediately, I was struck by the ostentatious opulence within. The most formal room in the house, the creams and blues of its decoration contrasted with the darkness outside. It was clear that the residents enjoyed luxuriating here with their guests. Four gilt-edged chairs with patterned cushions sat on each side of an imposing desk. The walls were paneled, and the back wall was dissected by a large grandfather clock in its center. I glanced at the time. Two o'clock? Surely it could not be that late?

A quick mental check confirmed my suspicion: the time was wrong. At the bottom of the clock face was a small panel showing the day of the week. It was marked Wednesday, and I was certain that this was incorrect, too. The clock must have been set to this specific time. The clock face itself was unusual in design: letters were written in front of each of the numerals, which made no sense to me at this stage.

I ducked out of the room to face my final open door: the bedchamber.

I peered in through the crack in the door, once again nervous about imposing my presence on anyone within. The room seemed remarkably impersonal. A four-poster bed was the center point. At the foot of it was a small sofa to lounge upon. Two chests of drawers sat on the opposite wall to the entrance. As much as it pained me, I decided to sneak a look inside of them. Missing something important based solely on my preconceived notions of what was polite and what wasn't was not an option.

The drawers were remarkably empty, except for some sewing supplies and a travel itinerary. Indeed, the itinerary implied that the family was away from home, visiting relatives in Loughborough. In which case, who had set up this situation, and how had they managed to time it so precisely for when the family was away?

A sense of foreboding came over me. Whatever was going on here had involved significantly more advanced planning than the simple opportunism that I had presumed.

My attention was drawn back to the bed itself. The linen was a most unusual design—a tapestry of different patterns. These had some repeats and did not seem to be in a specific order, but the patterns certainly reminded me of something that I had seen before. I took a mental note of the imagery and headed back out of the room and downstairs to the map. I needed to determine where the items within this mansion had been leading me.

It took me some time, but revisiting those six rooms gave me four instructions that I could use on the map. But in which order did I need to follow them? I gave a wry smile. Something told me I was right.

Once I had my four instructions and used them successfully on the map, I knew I could proceed.

HINTS
Difficult, turn to page 182
Medium, turn to page 187
Easy, turn to page 193
For solutions, turn to page 202

I must admit, I perhaps spent too long trying to determine if anything I had seen or done so far had given me the order for these instructions. I could have entered the rooms in almost any sequence and solved the conundrums equally randomly, so my own series of discovery could not have been a factor. Suddenly, I realized that I would end up in the same square, no matter in which order I traveled. Tracing the route with my finger led to a square, and as I tapped it to confirm to myself, I saw part of the word "Homestead" written through it.

"Homes."

Not exactly Sherlock's spelling, but it was a play on words that I suspected was deliberate. The square was centered on a tree that stood just outside the building. I picked up my hat, straightened my coat, and hurried outside, newly confident.

I approached the tree and immediately felt an unusual change of texture underfoot. After the front yard's grass, I was now standing on wood. Looking down, I could see, hidden underneath some leaves and grass shavings, a rope attached to a trapdoor. A secret entrance to the mansion's basement that I was unable to access from inside! What terrors could be hidden within? What was I meant to find?

I heaved the door open with the thick rope and stared down. Stone steps flickered in candlelight. It seemed

I was expected, and someone had gone to great lengths to reveal the tunnel underground. I traversed the cold stone to reach a wooden door, which I pushed open. Wine barrels encircled a dirty wooden table. An outstretched arm cradled a glass of red wine. As I approached from behind the tall-backed chair, a croak emerged: "You're here. And just on time."

I crossed the room to see who was there—the architect of my travels and the man behind Sherlock Holmes's disappearance. My eyes widened as I came face to face with the figure.

Holmes was sitting in the chair, as casually as if it were in his own home.

"My goodness, Holmes, whatever are you doing here?" I blurted out, a little put out by his nonchalance and brazen calm. "I thought that you had been abducted."

"What do you take me for, Watson?"

"I took you for someone that would not lead me on a merry goose chase."

"Watson, all of my steps were necessary, and fruitful, I promise you that. I will explain everything, but first I need your assistance."

"You could have asked me back in London," I retorted.

"But I could not, dear friend. My safety was not guaranteed and, frankly, I could not trust anyone, not even myself."

"I do not understand," I said, shaking my head.

"That has never stopped you before," Holmes replied, smiling. "Now, I have prepared a concoction that is important for you ingest."

"Ingest? Given your history, I am not sure that I trust what you want me to consume."

"Nonsense."

Holmes brought a new glass out from under his chair and thrust it into my eyeline. He tilted it toward me, and the questionable liquid flowed swiftly into my mouth. I was filled with confusion at his rapid movements and instinctively swallowed. The taste was acrid and bitter. I instantly retched but managed to keep the mixture down.

"What was that, Holmes?" I asked nervously.

"It will put you into a state of mental awareness that I consider close to my own usual thought processes. It will help me to prompt you with information and have you think it through in a way close to how I would. It may take some time, but we should reach the correct conclusions."

My vision became blurry, and I shook free from the man in the room. Surely, he could not be the Holmes I knew.

"What is it doing to me?"

"It is taking you somewhere, Watson."

"I do not understand. Where is it taking me?"

"To my mind palace, my friend."

I looked directly up and into his eyes. His sincerity calmed me as I lost consciousness and allowed myself to enter his world.

CHAPTER FOUR

The Mind Palace

What can I say about where I found myself next? Had I woken here, or had I fallen asleep to find myself here? Either way, here I was: inside a beautiful, awe-inspiring temple that resembled a golden version of the wondrous Taj Mahal. The sky was a swirl of curves and lines, warping and folding back in on themselves. Of course, I realized, Holmes had drugged me.

His booming voice echoed in my head, reminding me of a priest giving a sermon. "I have reduced your consciousness to thought. Merely your imagination and my words, combining to help you see what I should be able to see. The answer is in here somewhere, but beyond me at present. It is up to you now, Watson."

Could he hear me? Was I speaking out loud, with every thought? This situation frightened me, but as I seemingly could not immediately escape, I had no other choice than to attempt what he was pushing me toward.

"It started at the Falls," Holmes's voice boomed.

Instantly, water rushed over the top of the temple, obliterating my view; Holmes's words were coming to life. I was mesmerized by the lines of the water, rippling even as they fell, and traced them upward to the roof. Suddenly, it was no roof but instead the Reichenbach Falls in Switzerland. Two figures were wrestling on a ledge above me. It had to be Holmes and Professor Moriarty. I saw a hat dislodged in the struggle falling down toward the rocks below. It split into pieces, each forming the shape of another hat as they cascaded to the bottom.

I looked back up and both figures had disappeared. The water below me began to spread out, losing its deference to the laws of gravity, its pigments spreading as if light were shining through a prism. The colors seemed to settle on the canvas of the sky into recognizable patterns, as if they were paint in one of my friend's paintings. Somehow, Sherlock Holmes stepped out from behind a splatter of paint, still wearing his deerstalker. It must have been Moriarty's hat dislodged at the Falls.

The Mind Palace

He began to speak. "Watson, dear friend, it is important that you understand how my mind works so that you can make the same connections as I do. For me, colors are everything. Sounds, feelings, actions, and even words relate to colors, and these colors then relate back to feelings. Seeing connections in seemingly unrelated links comes through them. I believe the term coined for this is *synesthesia*."

I tried to speak back, but my mind was awash with the combination of sights and sounds, and I found myself happy to relax into what was being shown to me. My mind, however, was heading down a darker path. The paintlike splatters began changing, becoming darker and darker until they were entirely black, forming silhouettes over a blank white canvas in front of me.

"Unfortunately, some of these colors in particular evoke terrible feelings within me. Overwhelming, devastating, incorrigible feelings. Pain I have no choice but to numb in various ways."

The black pools became dark red. Blood red. On top of each was a figure. No, a body. A victim of some kind of accident or murder. His voice began naming each one:

"M. Franko, P. Lappel, B. Bolton . . ."

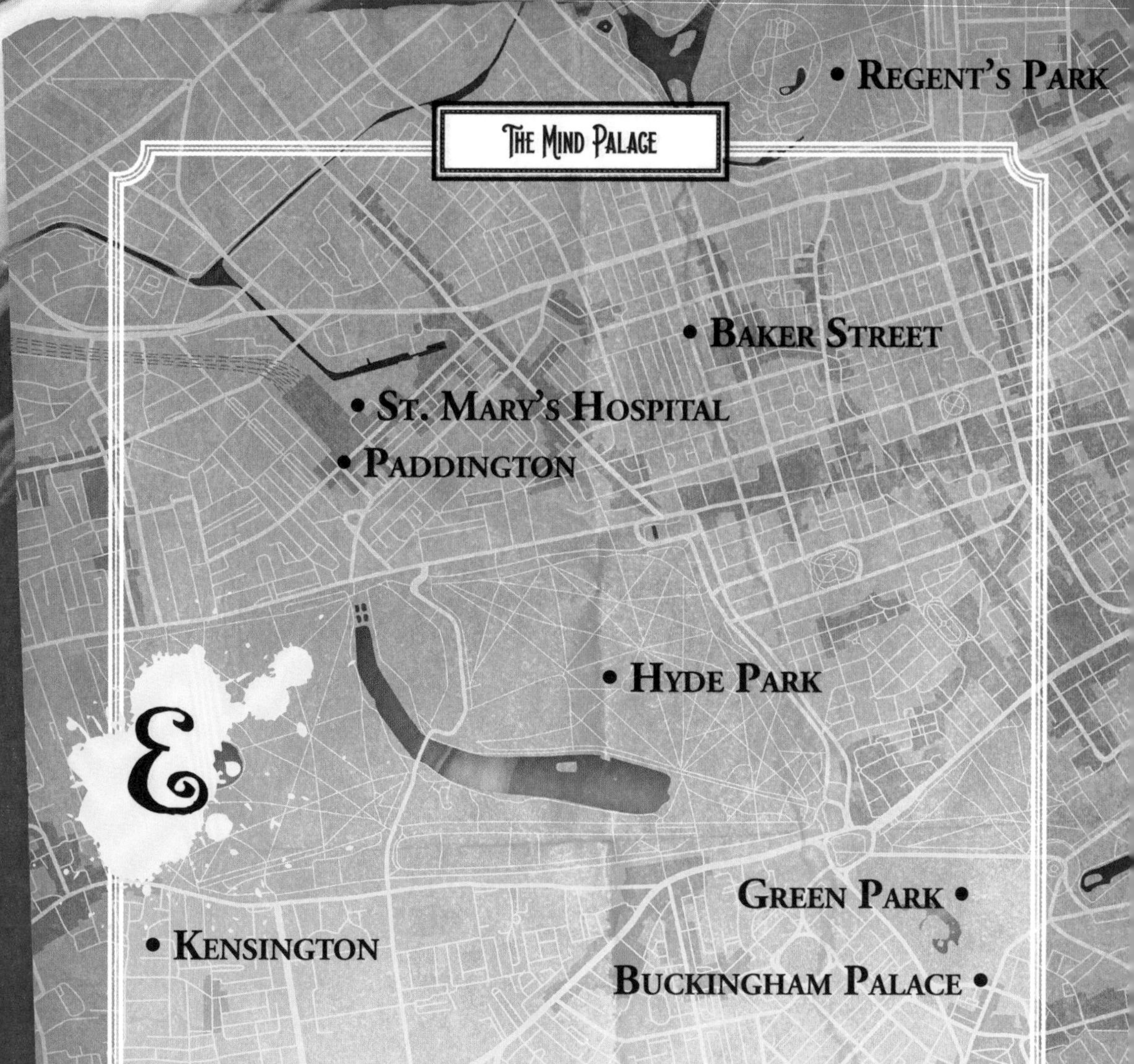

REGENT'S PARK •

• BAKER STREET

• ST. MARY'S HOSPITAL
• PADDINGTON

&

• HYDE PARK

GREEN PARK •

• KENSINGTON

BUCKINGHAM PALACE •

I found this experience to be truly uncomfortable, and I felt a sense of dread that knocked me for six. However, I also experienced a new feeling: it was as though I could sense a relationship between the body sizes, the colors of the bodies, the patterns on them, and the letters within each of their names. If I could figure out what each meant, then I might understand the pattern a little better.

A sudden whisper drew me away from my focus.

"London."

I could not tell whose voice it was, maybe it was my own, but it made me think of the city I called home. Holmes was pointing me toward somewhere in London. I tried to imagine important locations, but while many ideas came to mind, I could not immediately sense from his cues where to look.

• BATTERSEA PARK

Looking down, I perceived a map that had emerged beneath my feet. I saw Holmes over in Baker Street. He looked up at me and spoke some words that did not seem to make any sense contextually.

"Cat. Spade. Knife. Pipe. Heart. Umbrella."

The words became the items themselves, and they spun around each other, picking up other objects as they flew past my head. The thought crossed my mind that the items related to a case that I had written extensively about. A murder that, if memory served me correctly, Inspector Lestrade had mentioned in passing one time. When Holmes informed him that there was more to the case than met the eye, Lestrade had been insistent that it was open and shut. Perhaps it had been picking at Holmes's brain since then, or further connections had reminded him of it? But his mind was in no state to be making these connections nor, seemingly, would his memory allow for him to recall the details. That was my obligation now.

I looked around at the colors that had recently been formless shapes and could now see stained-glass windows, angular and glowing, joining to create the shape of a giant insect. Along each strut holding the windows up were small circular shapes, growing and shrinking. They seemed to my mind like mice, finding holes and entrances to dart in and out of. Then a flurry of hats washed over my vision.

• WESTMINSTER

• ARCHBISHOP'S PARK

• ST. JOHN'S CHURCH

• KENNINGTON

• THE OVAL

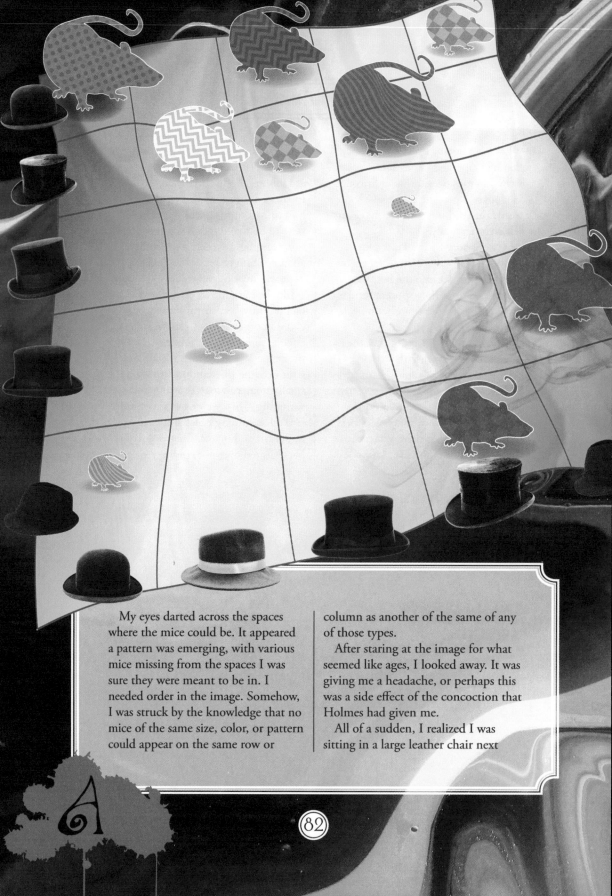

My eyes darted across the spaces where the mice could be. It appeared a pattern was emerging, with various mice missing from the spaces I was sure they were meant to be in. I needed order in the image. Somehow, I was struck by the knowledge that no mice of the same size, color, or pattern could appear on the same row or column as another of the same of any of those types.

After staring at the image for what seemed like ages, I looked away. It was giving me a headache, or perhaps this was a side effect of the concoction that Holmes had given me.

All of a sudden, I realized I was sitting in a large leather chair next to Holmes. A quick glance around confirmed that we were in an opium den. Rich red curtains flowed around us. While Holmes seemed to be speaking, I could no longer understand the words. He revealed an envelope from inside his jacket and presented it. The name on the front was illegible to me, but I went ahead and opened it to reveal the letter inside anyway, because that appeared to be his intention.

Although the words made no sense to me, I was able to understand its content. It was a job offer for a position somewhere in London to a man who lived far away, in the country. His abilities had been heard of far and wide, and the amount offered in remuneration seemed obscene and certainly impossible to refuse. It seemed too good to be true. I was certain there was more to this offer than simply a job.

I looked up and realized Holmes was praying, a somewhat unusual sight. He had been repeating "Amen" over and over the entire time.

"Amen," he insisted.

I could not decipher his purpose.

"Amen," Holmes bellowed.

But he was not praying.

"A man," Holmes clarified.

Of course. He was asking me to find the man. The man to whom the letter was addressed. I needed his name.

"And where?"

Holmes needed a lead from me. Not just the person in question but also where we needed to go to learn more. I felt myself falling. Everything faded around me until I could see only a few areas of color. This was all I was left with. There was only one way out. I needed a name and a place.

Once I had both of them, I knew I could proceed.

HINTS

Difficult, turn to page 183

Medium, turn to page 187

Easy, turn to page 193

For solutions, turn to page 206

"Bolton . . . St. Mary's," I chanted.

"Thank you, my friend," Sherlock replied warmly.

"Bolton . . . I'm . . . awake?"

My consciousness had returned me to the wine cellar where I had found Holmes. I was slumped in his chair, slightly confused but energized, a cold sweat beading down my forehead. I was feeling more awake and aware than ever before.

"How do you feel, Watson?"

"Remarkable."

"Quite right."

"It is as if a great weight has been removed from me. Somehow, I feel better than I would have felt had the weight not been placed upon me in the first place."

"Thank you for trusting me."

"As always, Holmes, I do not believe I had much of a choice."

He smiled.

"So," I began, lowering my voice. "What just happened?"

"You may well have solved what I could not."

"I did?"

"Bolton at St. Mary's. The connections were there, but I simply could not see them."

"Why could you not?"

"My medication. Necessary, yet damaging to my senses. Not permanently, I must hope, but my mind is dulled and what is happening as we speak may be time-sensitive. This is why I needed your help. I assumed that putting you into a state that would closely emulate my mind palace would help you to think in the same way, if I fed you the information I had."

"That *was* you?" I questioned. "All of the visions I had. The opium den, the bodies, the mice?"

"To an extent," Holmes said, clearly withholding the full details.

"So, what's really going on here?"

"Oh, I don't know yet. What you just went through was simply to determine the edge of this mystery; somewhere for us to begin, not the final unraveling."

"I don't understand."

"Neither do I, Watson. And isn't that the fun of it?"

I wanted to ask more, but the adrenaline I had felt on waking was waning and my limbs were weighed down through tiredness. I could not prevent myself from yawning.

"It looks as if you have had quite enough for today. Perhaps you should find a room upstairs and turn in for the night. We have a long day ahead tomorrow."

"What are we doing?"

"We are returning to London, and our first stop: St. Mary's Hospital."

I wanted more answers, but Holmes maintained a smug, knowing silence.

"I don't understand why you are so far from London now, in an out-of-the-way place like Cookham."

"Patience, my dear friend. We have enough time to answer that tomorrow. Go to bed."

"And you?" I asked.

"I have work to do. There is still a good portion of this bottle to finish."

I smiled, happy to see my friend alive and seemingly well, although tiredness insisted I retire to a bed for the night. I only hoped our partnership would be more successful, and perhaps conventional, tomorrow.

———◆◆◆———

A rapping on my chamber door awoke me. I had not achieved much slumber, but it happened that the knocking caught me at a period where I was not conscious.

"Watson, we have to go."

Holmes's voice permeated through the door. I smiled, the comfort of some element of normalcy giving me a positivity I had not felt for a while.

"I will just be a moment," I spluttered.

I gathered my things and, having no time to prepare myself for the day, I emerged from the room that I had claimed as my own more disheveled than I would have liked, but ready for our trip. He met me at the bottom of the stairs, sprightly and enthused.

"I trust you slept well?" I asked.

"At this point, more sleep will do me little good."

"That may be true for you . . ." I retorted.

"Come on, Watson. It is just a short walk from The Mount."

We departed the mansion and walked down the path. I wondered how Holmes had garnered the keys for this house.

"You are probably wondering how I came about having permission to use the house."

His deduction skills were still far above average.

"It is quite simple, my dear friend."

"Go on," I probed.

"One does not need permission, if one is aware of when the only living family members are away."

Holmes had used his knowledge of the Harris case that we solved in May 1887—and the family's vacation plans—to create his own safe location with no link to him. I wondered why he had gone to such lengths. We arrived at the carriage from last night and, once again, the boy got in with us. Holmes nodded at me, then at the boy. I was confused at this and studied him as we returned to Cookham railroad station.

Toward the end of the journey, Holmes leaned over to me and said: "Find a little something for the boy, won't you, Watson?"

"Do you mean money?"

He arched an eyebrow, knowingly. "No, something else to remember us by. That he can keep. Did you not bring anything other than your essentials?"

My mind searched and landed on Holmes's painting, which I had packed. Would he be willing to give it to the boy?

"Perfect. I believe he is a budding artist," he said.

The boy was pleased and studied the artwork closely until we arrived at the station. Holmes gave some money to our driver and shook his hand before we took up our positions on the station platform. We stood in silence, although not through my choice; every time I attempted to start a conversation, he halted me, insisting that this was not the place. Eventually, the train arrived, we boarded, and found our compartment. Finally, Holmes was able to unleash what had clearly been on his mind some time.

"Watson, my dear man, ever since the Reichenbach Falls, I have been unwell. The pain from my injuries, although not life-threatening, has been unbearable. I needed to dull it and, in doing so with the medication given to me, I dulled my own senses. I could not make the connections I normally would, but something troubled me. The information I gave you last night that led us to where we are going was not clear to me other than with a deep-seated feeling of unease and, dare I say it, dread."

"I see," I replied, in what I hoped was a reassuring manner.

"I realized there might be a time element to everything, however, when I saw a man following me with clearly less than positive intentions. It was apparent that while I could not surmise the solution myself, the mystery would have to be solved and, more important, I had to escape. My life was in danger, but from whom I am simply unaware."

"So, you need me for this case?"

"My dear Watson, I always need you. Just rarely to solve anything."

The journey to Maidenhead and on to London Paddington was a smooth one, despite Holmes's paranoia. We were untroubled by locked doors or insistent ticket collectors on our route back; Holmes assured me that they were never present on this route, despite my knowledge to the contrary. Upon arrival, we took a short walk to St. Mary's Hospital, where Holmes immediately advanced on the nurse on duty.

"Excuse me, my name is Sherlock Holmes and this is Dr. John Watson. I need to see the records of Mr. B. Bolton."

"I'm sorry, you can't just come barging in here demanding records."

"What my esteemed colleague means is that we have a meeting with Mr. Bolton's doctor about his records," I interjected.

"Who was that?"

"Well, he had a number of doctors, given his illness," I improvised. Holmes, seeming impressed, took a step back and allowed me to continue.

"His illness?" the nurse questioned.

"I am afraid that I am not at liberty to disclose his personal information," I replied quickly.

"Well, the last doctor to see him was Dr. Mansfield."

"He will be the one we need then."

"I'll get him down to see you."

"That's most kind," Holmes interjected.

I could not tell whether or not Holmes was enjoying taking a back seat, but he smiled at me as we walked away to sit and await the doctor. He remained close to the receptionist desk, examining the hospital map behind it. The doctor emerged not long after.

"You'll be wanting to see the operating room?" the man began, without so much as an introduction. "This way."

I turned around to look at Holmes, who seemed to not even be listening and was reaching over the desk instead. Both the doctor and myself looked at him quizzically.

"Mint, anyone?" Holmes asked, placing what he had claimed from behind the desk into his pocket. I shook my head as the doctor turned and led us away.

We followed, unquestioning. Had we stumbled upon something that others had noticed was unusual, or was the doctor expecting someone else? He held the door and ushered us inside. After a few steps, the overwhelming chemical smell hit me, and I turned around to ask what had happened with Mr. Bolton.

I was faced with the face of the doctor, resigned to an action that seemed to fill him with anger. He slammed it shut, and locked us in.

Holmes saw my nervousness at the situation and raised a hand to stop me from lunging at the door.

"Why do you not seem worried?" I asked my friend.

"Because, Watson, this tells me that we have arrived at the right place."

Sherlock Holmes and I were imprisoned in an operating room, but somewhere inside it lay the answers we needed.

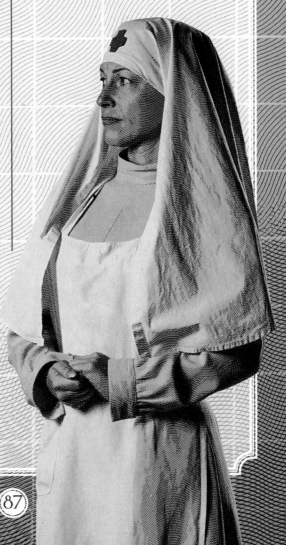

CHAPTER FIVE

THE OPERATING ROOM

My initial instinct was to double-check that the slammed door was indeed locked, but I decided this was unnecessary. Holmes's calm demeanor served to reassure me that everything was, if not going perfectly to plan, within the realm of acceptably chaotic.

My friend was not at that moment overly engaged with investigation. Instead, he was staring up at the ceiling at something I could not ascertain. I moved to speak to him, but he waved me away.

"I do believe that a full search of our vicinity may be of use here, Watson," he mused distractedly.

I smiled and shook my head. It was good to have my friend back.

Why were we here? That was my prime concern. The name Mr. B. Bolton had led us to this operating room, where, I presumed, the man had been under the care of that doctor. What had happened to him, and where was he now? I thought back to the map of London that I had so recently imagined. Perhaps one of those other locations would be our next stop?

Glancing around, there seemed almost too much to examine quickly for one person, and yet Holmes was still staring upward without a hint of helping me. I followed his gaze but could not determine the significance of what he was intrigued by—it appeared to be a pipelike drain above us. Why would there be a drain in an operating room? Where would its contents fall? The dirty tiles below it appeared to provide the answer. It had obviously been some time since they had been cleaned, and the pathways between the tiles had been blocked by someone for some obscure reason. There were also numbers and letters scrawled around the area.

Standing at the center of the room was, of course, a table. A patient would lie there while experts surrounded them, debating the best course of action, before attempting to heal them. A machine for administering an anesthetic was positioned nearby, the substance a relatively recent addition just a few decades ago. The removal of pain allowed for a more gentlemanly process. While my expertise as a physician lay not in the various methods and proportions necessary to administer it successfully, I could see a chart across the room, next to a collection of bottles and containers, that would assist with it.

"Trying to numb the pain, Watson?" Sherlock quipped.

"Actually, I would have thought anesthetic would be more down your street, Holmes."

"My injuries are subsiding. I am only taking what is necessary."

"No, I mean because of the origins of the word."

"Enlighten me."

"Well, the person who came up with the term *anesthesia* was a gentleman named Oliver Wendell Holmes. Unrelated to you, I assume?"

"I cannot confirm that he is," he replied, raising an eyebrow.

I wandered over and took a brief look at the mathematics that determined the usage of each substance for each body weight, but I didn't linger long enough to work out the correct quantities to use.

DETERMINING THE CORRECT AMOUNTS OF ANESTHETIC REQUIRES KNOWING YOUR PATIENT'S WEIGHT IN IMPERIAL, WHERE 1 STONE = 14 POUNDS, SO A 116-POUND PATIENT WEIGHS 8 STONE 4 POUNDS. ONCE YOU KNOW IT, WE CAN CONTINUE TO CALCULATE COCAINE, NITROUS OXIDE, AND ETHER IN THE CORRECT AMOUNTS. FOR SIMPLICITY'S SAKE, EACH INGREDIENT IS CONSIDERED IN TERMS OF THE NUMBER OF "UNITS" OF EACH SUBSTANCE.

----

* Cocaine must be used in the ratio of 3 units of cocaine to 2 units of ether.

* To calculate the units of ether to use, halve the pounds of the patient's weight and take that number off the number of stones that they weigh. For example, 8 stone 4 pounds would be 8 - 2 = 6.

* We need a certain number of units of nitrous oxide, which must be created by heating ammonium nitrate. To calculate how much nitrous oxide we need, we must add the numerical value of stones and pounds together.

* 12 units of ammonium nitrate create one unit of nitrous oxide. Calculate the amount needed. This will be a large number. I advise adding 20 extra units of ammonium nitrate, since some will be lost in the process.

* To collect the nitrous oxide, the ammonium nitrate must be bubbled through a trough, surrounded by water. The amount of water to use is directly relative to the amount of ammonium nitrate used. Divide the units of ammonium nitrate by 10 and round down.

* Add the numerical value of stone and pounds together to get the first number. It is safer to slightly overestimate weight so that the patient does not regain sensation during the procedure, so add one to the first number to get the second number.

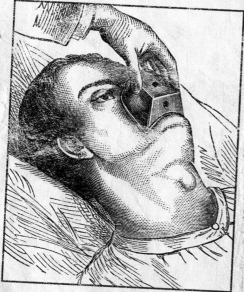

* The third number is the number of units of ether.

* The fourth number is the number of units of cocaine.

* The fifth number is a third of the number of units of water used.

* The sixth number is the number gained by adding up all of the digits in the units of ammonium nitrate used.

* The seventh number is the number of units of nitrous oxide.

* Take these numbers, and only a true AI student will understand their relevance.

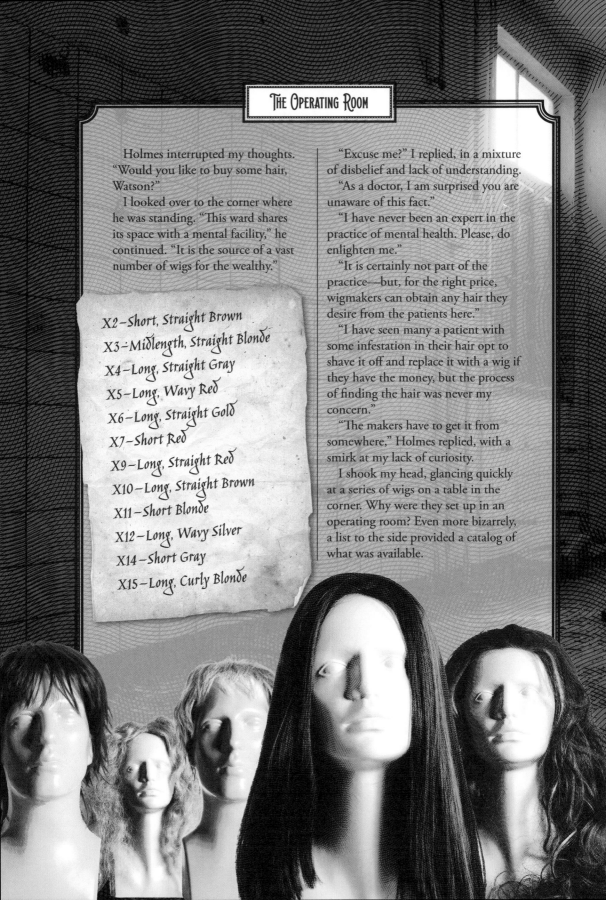

Holmes interrupted my thoughts. "Would you like to buy some hair, Watson?"

I looked over to the corner where he was standing. "This ward shares its space with a mental facility," he continued. "It is the source of a vast number of wigs for the wealthy."

X2–Short, Straight Brown

X3–Midlength, Straight Blonde

X4–Long, Straight Gray

X5–Long, Wavy Red

X6–Long, Straight Gold

X7–Short Red

X9–Long, Straight Red

X10–Long, Straight Brown

X11–Short Blonde

X12–Long, Wavy Silver

X14–Short Gray

X15–Long, Curly Blonde

"Excuse me?" I replied, in a mixture of disbelief and lack of understanding.

"As a doctor, I am surprised you are unaware of this fact."

"I have never been an expert in the practice of mental health. Please, do enlighten me."

"It is certainly not part of the practice—but, for the right price, wigmakers can obtain any hair they desire from the patients here."

"I have seen many a patient with some infestation in their hair opt to shave it off and replace it with a wig if they have the money, but the process of finding the hair was never my concern."

"The makers have to get it from somewhere," Holmes replied, with a smirk at my lack of curiosity.

I shook my head, glancing quickly at a series of wigs on a table in the corner. Why were they set up in an operating room? Even more bizarrely, a list to the side provided a catalog of what was available.

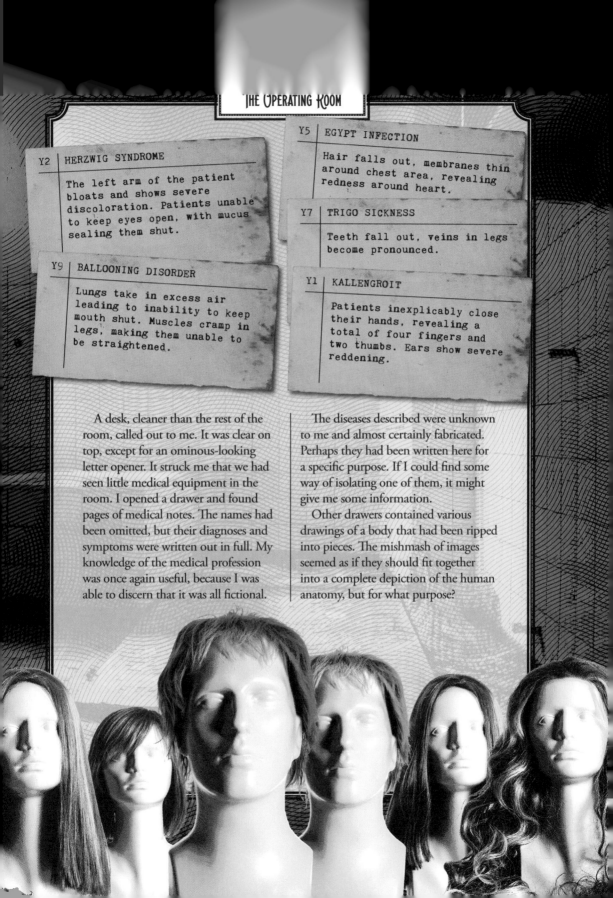

Y2 | HERZWIG SYNDROME

The left arm of the patient bloats and shows severe discoloration. Patients unable to keep eyes open, with mucus sealing them shut.

Y9 | BALLOONING DISORDER

Lungs take in excess air leading to inability to keep mouth shut. Muscles cramp in legs, making them unable to be straightened.

Y5 | EGYPT INFECTION

Hair falls out, membranes thin around chest area, revealing redness around heart.

Y7 | TRIGO SICKNESS

Teeth fall out, veins in legs become pronounced.

Y1 | KALLENGROIT

Patients inexplicably close their hands, revealing a total of four fingers and two thumbs. Ears show severe reddening.

A desk, cleaner than the rest of the room, called out to me. It was clear on top, except for an ominous-looking letter opener. It struck me that we had seen little medical equipment in the room. I opened a drawer and found pages of medical notes. The names had been omitted, but their diagnoses and symptoms were written out in full. My knowledge of the medical profession was once again useful, because I was able to discern that it was all fictional.

The diseases described were unknown to me and almost certainly fabricated. Perhaps they had been written here for a specific purpose. If I could find some way of isolating one of them, it might give me some information.

Other drawers contained various drawings of a body that had been ripped into pieces. The mishmash of images seemed as if they should fit together into a complete depiction of the human anatomy, but for what purpose?

A wooden filing cabinet in a corner drew me over. It was full of medical records. I thumbed through the index to find if B. Bolton was contained within. There was an entry! Perhaps this would be our starting point.

"I'm afraid you will not find our friend there, Watson."

"You have already taken a gander?"

"I have. His records are nowhere to be found."

Despite my friend's insistence, I looked anyway. He was correct, of course. Bolton's records were not there, but there were several others inside his file. Surely, they must have been important. Perhaps this obvious fact had passed Holmes by.

"Holmes, you did not mention these records."

"Well, if I had, you might not have looked at them so closely. There is plenty of information on them, yet nothing I think we can use until we have discovered the relevance of the other items in this room."

"And we need to know what happened to B. Bolton, or at least where to find him?"

"Astutely summarized, Watson."

I looked over everything we had found.

Once I'd worked out where to head next, I knew I could proceed.

HINTS

Difficult, turn to page 183
Medium, turn to page 188
Easy, turn to page 194
For solutions, turn to page 209

ID Number: 409
Name: **Mrs. S. Hapton**
Weight: 9 st. 2 lb.
Height: 4 ft. 11 in.
Hair: Long Blonde
Eyes: Blue

ID Number: 304
Name: **Ms. N. Shepherd**
Weight: 8 st. 4 lb.
Height 5 ft. 1 in.
Hair: Long Brown
Eyes: Hazel

ID Number: 262
Name: **Miss L. Ferrigamo**
Weight: 10 st. 12 lb.
Height: 5 ft. 4 in.
Hair: Medium Brown
Eyes: Blue

ID Number: 154
Name: **Mr. G. Brown**
Weight: 12 st. 10 lb.
Height: 5 ft. 8 in.
Hair: Short Gray
Eyes: Brown

ID Number: 223
Name: **Mr. F. Parfitt**
Weight: 14 st. 4 lb.
Height: 5 ft. 11 in.
Hair: Short Brown
Eyes: Green

ID Number: 857
Name: **Mr. R. Butcher**
Weight: 13 st. 6 lb.
Height: 6 ft.
Hair: Bald
Eyes: Brown

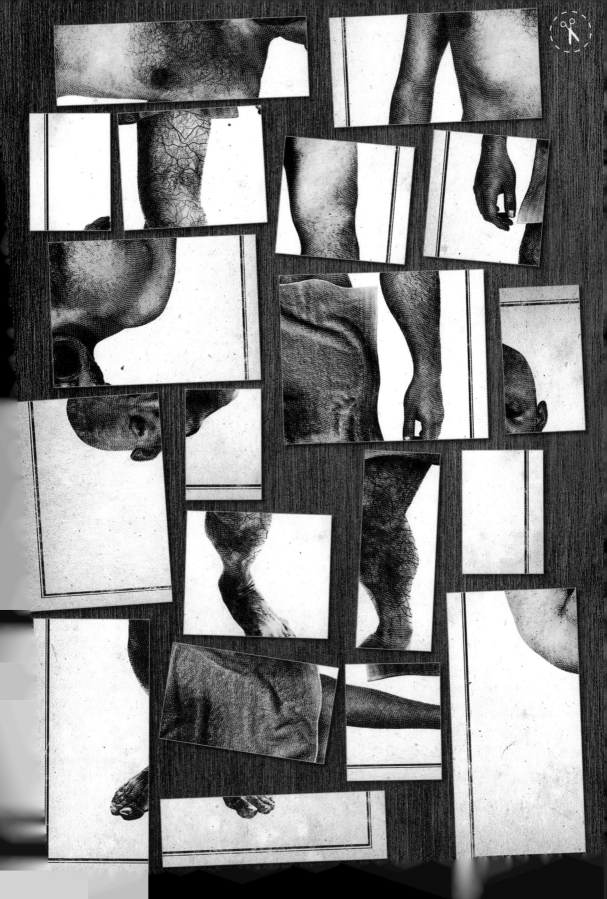

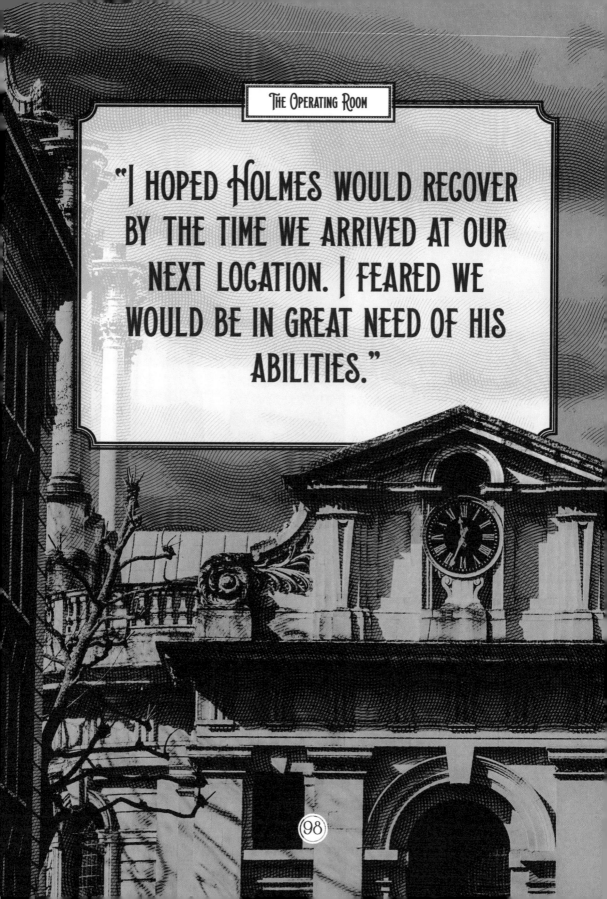

The Operating Room

"I HOPED HOLMES WOULD RECOVER BY THE TIME WE ARRIVED AT OUR NEXT LOCATION. I FEARED WE WOULD BE IN GREAT NEED OF HIS ABILITIES."

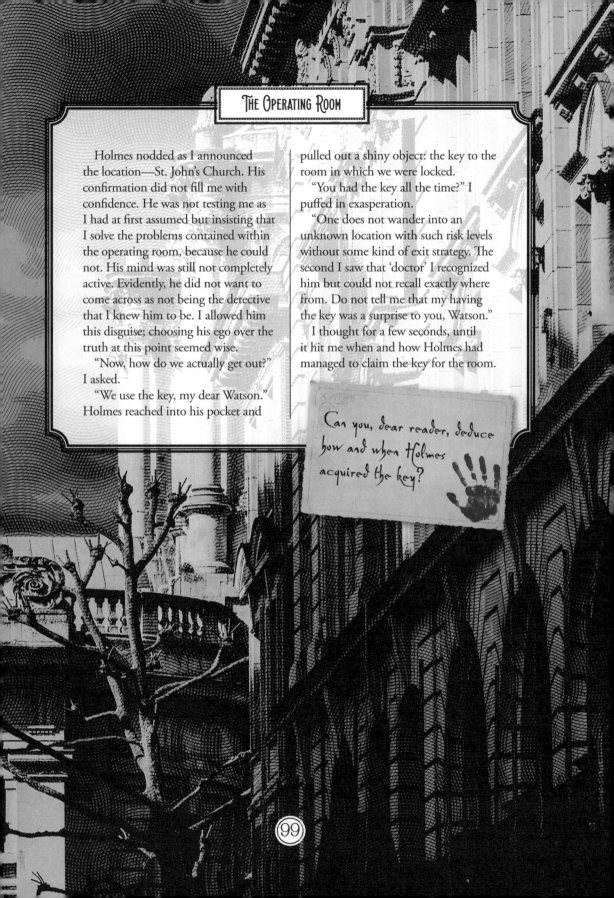

Holmes nodded as I announced the location—St. John's Church. His confirmation did not fill me with confidence. He was not testing me as I had at first assumed but insisting that I solve the problems contained within the operating room, because he could not. His mind was still not completely active. Evidently, he did not want to come across as not being the detective that I knew him to be. I allowed him this disguise; choosing his ego over the truth at this point seemed wise.

"Now, how do we actually get out?" I asked.

"We use the key, my dear Watson." Holmes reached into his pocket and pulled out a shiny object: the key to the room in which we were locked.

"You had the key all the time?" I puffed in exasperation.

"One does not wander into an unknown location with such risk levels without some kind of exit strategy. The second I saw that 'doctor' I recognized him but could not recall exactly where from. Do not tell me that my having the key was a surprise to you, Watson."

I thought for a few seconds, until it hit me when and how Holmes had managed to claim the key for the room.

Can you, dear reader, deduce how and when Holmes acquired the key?

Holmes had been standing near the reception desk, looking at the map of the hospital, probably where the keys had been stored. When the doctor arrived, he recognized him and, not knowing exactly from where, he feared the worst. Upon the doctor announcing that we would be heading to the operating room, Holmes made his move. He swiped a duplicate key, passing the action off as picking up a mint, which he happily announced to draw suspicion away from his action.

"Very clever," I acknowledged. "But why did you insist on keeping us in here all of this time?"

"The information we needed was inside. You found it. Only now do we need to leave. If I had played my card earlier, someone may have found the door unlocked and started asking questions. We may have lost our chance."

"Speaking of our chance, Holmes, perhaps we should take our leave and head to the church."

"Pope Leo will be proud of you, Watson," he smiled.

Having studied the map, Holmes had no trouble leading us out of the hospital through a quiet path, back to the entrance we arrived at. Taking a chance, he smiled at the receptionist and called out as we scuttled past.

"Thank you for your assistance."

A nod was all that was returned, and we'd been granted the freedom we hoped for. Outside, a carriage stood waiting and I hastened toward it. Holmes put his hand on my shoulder. "A waiting carriage has a purpose, and given that much of what is occurring at present seems to be part of a larger plan, I suggest that we leave on foot and procure a more fortuitous form of transportation."

He may have been overly cautious, or perhaps he was correct. Either way, it did not hurt to not take any chances at this point. A few streets from the hospital, we climbed into a carriage and proceeded on our way.

"You must be asking the same questions I am, Watson," Holmes began. "Why did we follow a name to St. Mary's Hospital and what did we learn there?"

"Quite right, Holmes. His name was nowhere, and yet we definitely found the right place."

"Why would his name not exist on any of the medical records that we found?"

"Because he is not a real person, Watson."

"I do not understand."

"Whatever medical procedure was carried out on that man, and whatever happened to him in that hospital, was meant to be hidden from us, so there were no records. I can only assume that

his real name, Mr. Butcher, must lead us to the next stage of this mystery, and someone at the church to which we are headed may know him."

"Or even be him," I added.

"Very true, my friend. We have established that names mean nothing on this journey. Anyone that we meet could be impersonating anyone else. Be on your guard."

I looked down at my shoes, still remarkably clean despite traipsing around the countryside and half of London, while Holmes's words resonated in my mind. His earlier paranoia, or what I assumed to be so due to his intoxicated brain, had turned out not to be unfounded. Until the doctor locked us up, there had been nothing untoward about our situation beyond Holmes's own designs, yet there could be no doubt now. We were headed deeper into the mystery, and every step took us potentially into more danger. Was finding the church a clever deduction, or were we meant to uncover it? Were we coming closer to the solution or walking into a trap? This did not matter to our next steps, of course. When a case had gripped Mr. Sherlock Holmes, there was no separating him from it, and even if I was not associated with the man, I would still be too intrigued to stop myself from investigating further.

Holmes was also in his own world, visibly straining in thought, and probably struggling with his own abilities. They did not appear to me to be that much less than usual, but any handicap obviously felt like a ball and chain weighing him down.

"I am not too proud to ask for your help, you know," he admitted.

"And I am not foolish enough to think that our partnership has ever been simply one way, Holmes," I acknowledged.

Holmes chuckled. "I am not my usual self, as you know, Watson. If we are to defeat whatever is afoot, we must accept our current roles. You know my mind better than any other. I can point you to the correct door, but it is you that will have to determine how to unlock it."

"I understand, my friend. I will do my best."

This seemed to satisfy him. For my friend, it was a remarkable admission of fallibility, and one that I would not allow to go uncomforted. This current situation must have caused a blow to his psyche and confidence, even if this was as much of it as he could show.

As we neared the church, I shouted to the driver to halt. If we were walking into a trap, I wanted a chance to approach unnoticed. Holmes nodded, seemingly proud of my foresight. We stepped out and looked around for any sign of observers or suspicious factors in our vicinity. It seemed reasonably clear. I paid the man and walked toward the main entrance. Holmes called out to me, still by the carriage. "Stop, man. We should take the less-exposed route."

He was right, of course. We wandered, as casually as we could to avoid arousing suspicion, around the grounds of the church and through

a back gate that opened into a walled area. It was a graveyard. Large statues and stones lined our clean, well-maintained path. Farther from the path, the stones became smaller and the ground muddy; status and wealth visible, even after death. A group of mourners were standing around a freshly filled plot. I squinted to see more, but Holmes shook his head at me. We were attempting to be inconspicuous, after all. We continued along the path until we reached the back entrance to the church. It was as grand as the front, yet with a smaller door cut into the large double doors. Holmes advanced first, grabbing the handle, turning it, and, with a sigh of surprise, pushing it open. He looked back at me silently, and with that I realized that stealth was still his plan.

We entered quietly and stood in the grand nave. No one was around. I opened my mouth to call out but thought better of it. We moved up toward the sanctuary and turned toward a small door to the side, which we tried quickly. Locked. We had turned to search further when we heard a muffled call from behind the door. Someone was in there.

"Are you all right, old chap?" I called, as softly as I could.

The muted sounds seemed to confirm a man in peril. We had to open the door. Out of interest—and fear—I jogged back to the entrance. My worries were confirmed. The door we had entered was unmoving.

We were locked within this church and had to discover not only how to free the man, but to escape ourselves.

CHAPTER SIX

THE CHURCH

"W atson," Holmes announced. "This is precisely why one should always plan ahead, as I did at the operating room."

"Have you already managed to find a key for this place, Holmes?" I replied, astonished at his apparent foresight.

"No, not me. The man locked in this church."

"I believe we are all locked in this church."

His silence could have been taken as somewhat touchy. However, I believe he may have been enjoying the repartee that he would otherwise have glossed over, had his mind been as it should. I took a few steps from Holmes, intending to undertake my own investigation. Whatever I thought of the man's usual demeanor, there was no denying his brilliance. Right now, however, it was my time to impress.

"No puzzle is unsolvable," I muttered to myself.

"That is not strictly true." Holmes's ears pricked up.

"Well, I suppose not. But perhaps no logical puzzle has no way of being approached."

"We shall see, shall we not, Watson?"

I could see only two solutions to the problem of releasing the man, although in reality they were two problems: releasing him and then releasing ourselves. I hoped that the former would assist in the latter. We could either find the key—perhaps a backup, stashed somewhere secret. Alternatively, we could attempt to remove the door from its hinges, but the brute-force solution seemed both inelegant behavior in a church and overly difficult considering the size and strength of the door. That left finding the key. Surely a place like this would have one hidden somewhere, but where?

Wandering between the pews, I was keeping my eyes open for any sign of storage when it struck me, like stepping outside into the cold. There was a donations box at the entrance, locked from behind with a three-digit number combination. Perhaps it was a sensible location to hide keys; secure enough that no one could stroll in and find them, yet open enough that any member of the church who needed access could memorize a number, or at least deduce the number from elsewhere.

"Have you noticed the somewhat unusual combination of obscurities about this place?" Holmes piped up.

"I have not had the chance to," I admitted.

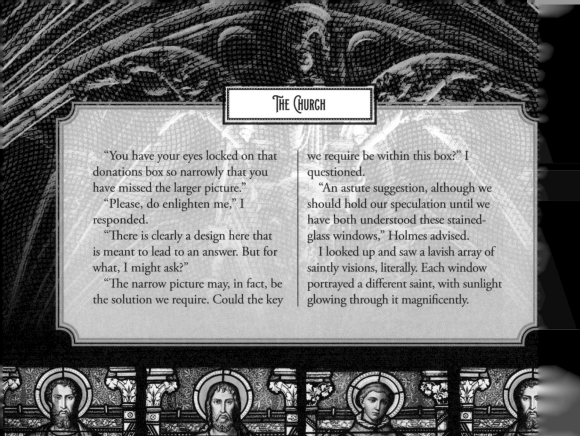

"You have your eyes locked on that donations box so narrowly that you have missed the larger picture."

"Please, do enlighten me," I responded.

"There is clearly a design here that is meant to lead to an answer. But for what, I might ask?"

"The narrow picture may, in fact, be the solution we require. Could the key we require be within this box?" I questioned.

"An astute suggestion, although we should hold our speculation until we have both understood these stained-glass windows," Holmes advised.

I looked up and saw a lavish array of saintly visions, literally. Each window portrayed a different saint, with sunlight glowing through it magnificently.

SAINT SIRICIUS   SAINT BENNO   SAINT FELIX   SAINT A

I stared up at the glass for so long that I lost my balance slightly. Holding out my hand to steady myself on a pew, I saw that the rows were marked with letters, and there were numbers spaced across each pew. Requiring specific seats when attending church seemed unusual, but perhaps it would be important. I made a quick sketch, hoping it would be helpful later.

At the far ends of the pews were four statues depicting various religious figures, I assumed, with two on each side of the church. All four of them were looking in different directions: left, right, up, and down. I stood by them and tried to follow their eyelines, but I could not determine anything unusual about what they could "see."

"Look here, Watson." I heard Holmes's voice echo through the cavernous building, at some distance from me; the acoustics were truly humbling.

"What is it, Holmes?"

"Take a look at this," he offered, pointing at a large musical organ as I approached. "What do you make of it?"

"There are letters on a number of the keys."

"Exactly right. And from the left to the right, whoever has marked this instrument has decided to refer to each set of eight notes as a different number, so the first, from C up to B, would be 1, the next 2, and so on."

"But they have decided to end it after the eighth octave."

"Indeed. Now, more interestingly than the notes being labeled is the color of four of the keys."

It was hard to miss, but I felt like Holmes needed the win. "Oh yes, I almost did not see them," I feigned.

"Do not treat me like an invalid, Watson. I know you cannot have missed them."

"So, what do they mean then?"

"If I knew that, we'd already have the key."

Directly opposite the organ was the pulpit. I decided to take a look and see if there was anything unusual there, or anything I could see from a different vantage point. Holmes must have had the same idea, and jauntily leaped in front of me. "Hurry up, Watson," he joked, infuriatingly.

Upon arrival, we found what seemed at first to be a Bible, bookmarked on several specific pages of various verses concerning the saints' actions.

Holmes made a somewhat too obvious humming noise and piped up: "My biblical knowledge is a trifle rusty, I fear, but this certainly does not ring any bells for me. I do not believe this to be a real Bible. The passages are not even connected to one another."

If correct, it would mean this book was important to our investigation. It could not have been left open by chance. Clues must be within.

THE SAMARITAN OF JERICHO

aint Alban was speaking to a group of travelers, who all had questions for him.

"Alban," they asked. "Why do you show us such kindness?"

"I show to you the same kindness that was given to me by Siricius. He would often give all that he had to me when he had little. Siricius did not even know me by name and yet all that was his was mine."

One of the travelers, named Felix, asked, "I passed through a town nearby and met a man who was lying by the side of the road. He would ask every time I saw him: 'Felix, I am ill and need medicine.' I had no medicine of my own, yet what else could I have done for this man Benno (for that was his name)?"

"Was Benno not your brother, as all men are your brothers? When a man, such as Benno, is in need, it is not for Benno or yourself that you help him. It is for God."

THE MUSICIAN

 talented musician named Felix played the flute and captivated the marketplace.

"Felix, play all day for my customers," demanded Siricius, the seller.

The musician replied, "I cannot play for your customers, Siricius, for bringing them would benefit you, by bringing them to you."

The wise old man Alban spoke up. "You play for neither his customers nor him."

"I do not understand, Alban," said the musician.

"Your talent shows me one thing. You are playing for your own pleasure. You play for you."

The Shepherd

 shepherd while tending his sheep met a man walking and asked for his name.

"My name is Felix, and while I give you my name freely, why do you ask?"

The shepherd was surprised at the question. "I do not find it unusual to ask someone's name, Felix. I give mine, Benno, as freely as you give yours."

The walker asked, "Then why do you not greet with your name, Benno, before asking for mine?"

"If I had begun with my own introduction, then perhaps your foreknowledge of me may have given you prejudice to avoid sharing yours."

"I imagine that if I were aware of you, Benno, it would be through far more than your name. The shepherd who tends his flock in his fields over here leaves little space for doubt. I ask, however, what you have to hide."

"It is by manner of protection that I do not share who I am when I have such a valuable flock."

"But Benno, now we are acquainted, your flock is safer."

The Wolf and the Eagle

 hile the wolf stalks the ground, the eagle stalks the air," Benno explained to his wife. "Although neither would be cause for concern of the other, they are both predators and both worried for their next meal."

"But Benno, is the eagle not above the wolf?"

"In many ways, it is, of course. Yet can they both exist without one another?" Benno replied. "The balance between the two could be the same as the balance between the farmhand and the owner. They are more likely to survive if they work together."

"I think I see, Benno," his wife replied.

Once I had the three-digit code, I knew I could proceed.

"I am certain that we can make some kind of sense from this nonsense," I confirmed.

"Well then, my dear Watson, I believe we are in your capable hands."

I thought for a while about what we had seen, sure that it would lead me to the code for the donations box and hopefully the way to release the man deeper within the church. But where to begin?

HINTS
Difficult, turn to page 184
Medium, turn to page 188
Easy, turn to page 194
For solutions, turn to page 211

My code was correct and the donation box opened. I will admit that I felt slightly ashamed at my actions, having only my educated guess that it contained what I sought. If someone came in now to find me, hand in the box, reaching around for what they must assume was a tithe, it would not look kindly on me. Fortunately, my hand came across a larger item than a coin; it was a key. Instantly, I whipped out the item and took a step toward where the man was locked. Only belatedly did I consider the church's security, and I returned the lock to its hasp before turning back to my objective.

"Impressive, Watson," Holmes complimented.

I sunk the key into its lock, then, happily discovering that it fit, turned it with a metallic thud and pushed the door open. We were confronted with the shocking sight of the priest, tied up on a large chair and gagged.

While I rushed to his aid, Holmes was more interested in looking around, I assumed for indications of what had happened here. I considered that asking the priest himself might give a better solution and removed his gag.

"Thank you, thank you!" he spluttered.

"What happened here?" I asked.

Holmes remained pensive and quiet, studying a calendar that was on the wall. Today's date was empty, no doubt the reason why we were the first to discover the priest.

"These men came and locked me in here. Are you Dr. Watson?"

"You have heard of me?" I said, pleased at the recognition.

"Only through the men that tied me up."

My ego took a small hit, but I nevertheless pursued my task. "Why were they here?"

"I don't know," the priest insisted. "They simply turned up, asked if a man fitting your description had been here yet, and muscled me into this chair."

I looked down at the chair and saw his shoes and the bottom of his pants were in a state, covered in mud. Perhaps the struggle had taken a toll on him.

"Did they hurt you?" I asked, motioning to the dirt.

"No, I performed a funeral in the grounds earlier."

"And they mentioned Watson by name?" Holmes interjected.

"That's right."

Holmes had seen something in what had been said. An ordinary man might have passed it over, but what had sparked his interest? Holmes held up a newspaper showing a picture of myself and him. A high-profile case had given us a bit of fame some time ago, yet this paper was still intact, and, more important, in this room.

"You know more than you are saying," Holmes insisted.

"Why would a priest hide anything from us, Holmes?" I asked.

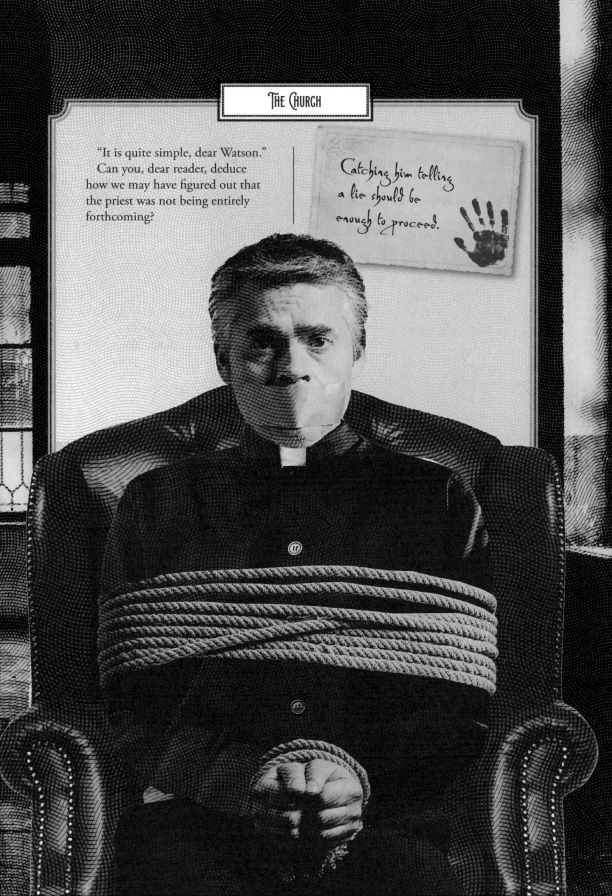

THE CHURCH

"It is quite simple, dear Watson."
Can you, dear reader, deduce
how we may have figured out that
the priest was not being entirely
forthcoming?

Catching him telling
a lie should be
enough to proceed.

Holmes began, "You say that you only know of Watson from the men that tied you up, yet the paper clearly shows both myself and him. Obviously, you had been told about Watson specifically and been shown the newspaper before being tied up. The reason for leaving the newspaper behind could have only been to help remind you of what he, or I, looked like so that you could perform some action in the future. Perhaps you were threatened to say only so much about what occurred here? Now, I can assure you that we will discover the truth, and stop whatever nefarious force is acting here, so you can either assist us in this matter and have us bring the criminals to justice quickly, or delay us in our ultimate goal and have the villains believe that you helped us anyway."

"There is little point, Holmes, in continuing this thread," I said, smiling.

"Of course there is. Any method of speeding up our investigation must be taken. We must know what he is hiding."

"We already do. I learned a little something from you, Holmes. The priest's shoes and pants look coated

ROVE 1891-1893

S. LIGHTS
1849-1854

P. GORDAN 1828-184

K. OCKNELL
1821-1822

L. PALMER
1841-1855

D. ABBEY
1842-1845

in dirt, and not the dirt of the path leading here. He has been in the grounds of the church, yet the calendar shows nothing on it. He had no funeral planned. You see the shovel behind him? He has been digging . . . deep in the graveyard."

I turned to the priest. "They made you . . . dig up a body?"

The priest burst into tears.

"They said they would kill my family if I refused."

"Excellent work, Watson," Holmes proudly announced.

"Whose grave did you dig up?"

The priest led us outside to the area of the graveyard. We were correct: he had been hiding something, and the front-door key was in his possession. He shook his head and pointed to a large crypt that had a series of numbers written on the side—they must be important.

"You opened up the crypt?" Holmes asked.

"No. I simply cannot recall which grave it was. It was the dead of night and there was only candlelight around.

F. HAMPTON
1887-1894

H. BEN
1882-

FRODSHAM
1831-1840

M. FAWLEY
1839-1851

B. HARRISON
1834-1842

SAVAGE
1850-1854

Q. JUPEST
1854-1860

G. RID
1836

The men ordered me to dig. The answers you seek w-will be h-here," the priest stuttered, pointing at the crypt.

"Watson, it must be one of the graves in this area," Holmes began. "It is all fresh soil here—recent burials—to hide the aforementioned actions. Interesting. There are exactly twenty-six graves. But I am convinced that we must start at the crypt."

Once I had decoded the numbers on the crypt and discovered which body had been dug up, I knew I could proceed.

T. GREEN 1825-1843

Z. ESERIN 1878-1894

R. SIMES
1833-1850

O. BUTLER
1847-1866

A. OLIVER
1837-1859

Y. SANDERS
1859-1885

N. PHYSICK
1851-1866

X. RUBENS
1871-1891

12 2 22 24 19 26

J. MCAVOY 1873-1894

V. OSMAN
1844-1868

W. HARRIS
1856-1879

I. SPARKS 1826-1851

"So, it seems that Bolton was a fake name, intended to mask the body's true identity. The identity of this J. McAvoy."

"But what does this tell us, Holmes?"

"That someone exhumed him, brought him to the hospital where we were so lavishly welcomed, and performed some kind of work on his body."

"Whatever for?"

"That, my dear Watson, is precisely what we must discover. I suggest we adjourn to visit a friend of ours to determine more about this victim."

As per his words, we left the priest to his own company and headed over to Scotland Yard, where we hoped Inspector Lestrade would assist us. Upon approach, Holmes was noticeably jumpy, which was unlike him. The situation was certainly causing him unrest. I suspected this was due to the unusual nature of what was occurring with him.

As soon as he was certain that no one had been following us, Holmes strode into the police station and bellowed his instructions to the officer on duty in the reception.

"I am here to see Inspector Lestrade."

"I'm sorry, sir, he's currently out on duty."

"Then I will wait right here until he returns."

J. McAvoy.

Why was it not B. Bolton? I was sure that name had led us here, and yet there was no sign of the man in question. Holmes seemed less disappointed than I.

"I must commend you, Watson," he began. "I was not expecting you to be so quick, and certainly not so successful in this time frame."

"Why would you doubt me, Holmes?"

"Why should I break the habit of a lifetime?"

I could tell by the glint in his eye that he was attempting to make a joke, but I confess I did not find it amusing. However, I still did not understand the relevance of the grave we had found.

"SOMEONE EXHUMED HIM, BROUGHT HIM TO THE HOSPITAL ... AND PERFORMED SOME KIND OF WORK ON HIS BODY."

"But it could be hours, sir."

"Or you could have very fortunate timing, Mr. Holmes," a voice called out from behind us.

We spun around to see Lestrade, resplendent in self-confidence and achievement.

"A successful case, Lestrade?" Holmes suggested.

"Indeed. We are in the business of police work, you know? When you are not around, crimes still get solved."

"How dreadfully dull that must be for you," Holmes retorted. "Anyway, I am hoping that you will be able to help us. What do you know about the recent murder of a J. McAvoy?"

"McAvoy, eh? That does ring a bell, actually. Why don't you come with me and we'll take a look at the case file."

Lestrade led the way, and we dutifully followed into the depths of Scotland Yard.

CHAPTER SEVEN

SCOTLAND YARD

L estrade opened the door to a large room with a huge table in the center. The walls were covered in standard law enforcement information: officers' patrol routes and schedules. There were sheets of paper covered in endless details, and a filing cabinet in the corner marked "Notable Persons" invited investigation.

"Here's everything we have on the McAvoy case," the inspector announced, flinging a folder of files across the table.

Papers flew out haphazardly, and Holmes's eyes seemed to light up.

"Do you have any suggestions on where to start?" I questioned.

"Unfortunately, Doctor, there is a reason why the case was on hand . . ."

"It's still open," Holmes interjected.

"Correct. We have no conclusions, and therefore no real starting point for you."

This seemed to please Holmes. Before we could ask anything else, there was a knock on the door. A small, well-dressed, bespectacled figure, whom I recognized as the chief superintendent, stuck his nose in.

"Lestrade, can I see you in my office, now? We can't hold Greaves any longer, and we're out of space in the cells."

"Of course, sir," he replied, turning back to us. "You've got an hour."

With no starting point, this was going to be an unusual investigation. I looked around the room, in the hope that something would stand out. I thought I should probably begin with the case file, which had a "confiscated items list" attached with illustrations drawn on it. A note on the back said that the police had returned an item to an innocent party.

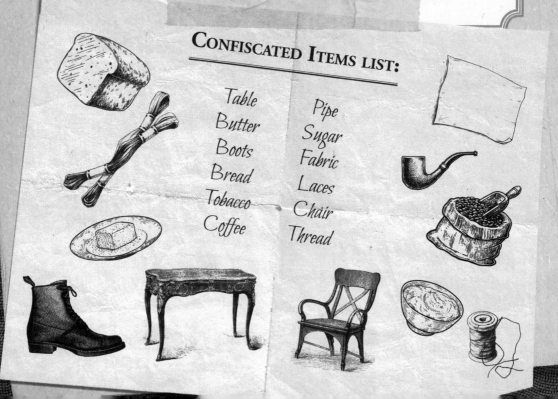

CONFISCATED ITEMS LIST:

Table
Butter
Boots
Bread
Tobacco
Coffee

Pipe
Sugar
Fabric
Laces
Chair
Thread

Name of Suspect:	Unknown
Alias:	Unknown
Address:	Unknown
Crime:	Murder
Victim:	Jack McAvoy
Age:	Unknown—approximately 20-30
Trade:	Wigmaker
Height:	6 ft. 1 in.
Weight:	143 lb.
Hair:	Brown
Eyes:	Blue
Investigating Officer:	Cameron Martin
Date of crime:	Sunday, June 18, 1894
Time of crime:	Unknown
Remarks:	Body was discovered by Officer C. Martin and Officer P. Trilby, who arrived at the scene at the same time through their regular patrols.

POLICE SCHEDULES—TIME TO PATROL IN EACH AREA (INCLUDING WALKING TIME TO NEXT AREA). TRY TO
ARRIVE AT THE EXACT TIME YOU'RE MEANT TO PATROL—E.G., TRILBY, ARRIVE AT WHITEHALL AT 07:40 A.M.

P. TRILBY PC 903/START TIME
7:00 A.M.
Scotland Yard Briefing 40 minutes
Patrol Whitehall 15
Patrol Parliament Street 17
Patrol Broad Sanctuary 28
Patrol Victoria Street 17
Patrol Palace Road 9
Patrol Grosvenor Gardens 8
Patrol Grosvenor Place 6
Patrol Hyde Park Corner 10
Patrol Piccadilly 65
Patrol Berkeley Street 22
Patrol Berkeley Square 8
Patrol Bruton Street 8
Patrol Berkeley Square 13

Patrol Mount Street 24
Patrol Park Lane 20
Patrol Hyde Park Corner 20
Patrol Palace Gardens 35
Patrol Bird Cage Walk 28
Patrol Great George Street 46
Patrol Parliament Street 41
Scotland Yard Debrief

C. MARTIN PC 495/START TIME
6:00 A.M.
Scotland Yard Briefing 38 minutes
Patrol Whitehall 35
Patrol Parliament Street 13
Patrol Bridge Street 21
Cross Westminster Bridge 18

Patrol Belvedere Road 25
Cross Charing Cross Bridge 20
Patrol Northumberland Avenue 10
Patrol Charing Cross 17
Patrol Whitehall 5
Patrol St. James' Park 18
Patrol Buckingham Palace 20
Patrol Green Park 28
Patrol Piccadilly 22
Patrol Old Bond Street 15
Patrol Bruton Street 10
Patrol Old Bond Street 15
Patrol Piccadilly 19
Patrol Green Park 41
Patrol St. James' Park 90
Scotland Yard Debrief

W. KHOJI PC 720/START TIME 8:00 A.M.
Scotland Yard Briefing 30 minutes
Patrol Whitehall 18
Patrol St. James Park 17
Patrol Buckingham Palace 19
Patrol Constitution Hill 28
Patrol Green Park 26
Patrol Piccadilly 10
Patrol Old Bond Street 17
Patrol Bruton Street 5
Patrol Berkeley Square 6
Patrol Hill Street 8
Patrol Union Street 25
Patrol South Audley Street 43
Patrol Mount Street 63
Patrol Park Lane 20
Patrol Hyde Park Corner 7

Patrol Grosvenor Place 21
Patrol Grosvenor Gardens 12
Patrol Victoria Street 71
Patrol Broad Sanctuary 22
Patrol Parliament Street 12
Scotland Yard Debrief

If we can work out the time period when the crime must have happened, based on where and when it was discovered, we may eliminate suspects.

CONNAUGHT ROAD

LONDON

A suspect spent all day on June 18 when he was not at work trying to remove this street sign from the wall. While we could not identify the person, there must be some way of working out what reason they had for wanting this sign. While this is a serious enough crime, the person could not have committed any other crimes on this day.

WANTED

Criminal known as "The Knife"

Robbed people at knifepoint: outside Buckingham Palace, on the center of Waterloo Bridge, at the meeting between Griffin St. and York Road, and at the meeting of St. James St. and King St.

Reward offered.

Captured on June 16, 1894—still locked up. Turns out his crimes formed an X on the map over his workplace. What a stupid mistake!

NOTABLE PERSON: LLOYD HARDIMAN

EMPLOYMENT: Horse Guards.
CRIMINAL RECORD: None.
ALIBI: 2-8 p.m., at work every day.
CELL NUMBER: 4

NOTABLE PERSON: MARK JOHNSON

EMPLOYMENT: Tobacconist.
CRIMINAL RECORD: Vandalization,
   Attempted murder, Horse theft,
   Soliciting.
ALIBI: 11 a.m.-6 p.m., at work
   every day.
CELL NUMBER: 1

NOTABLE PERSON: SHERLOCK HOLMES

EMPLOYMENT: Consulting Detective.
CRIMINAL RECORD: Not convicted of
   anything.
ALIBI: None. Does what he wants,
   when he wants.
CELL NUMBER: NA

NOTABLE PERSON: HARRY PRATT

EMPLOYMENT: National Gallery.
CRIMINAL RECORD: Evading arrest, Attempted
   murder, Horse theft.
ALIBI: 10 a.m.-1 p.m., at work every day.
CELL NUMBER: 2

DETAILED CRIME REPORT

DATE OF REPORT: June 15, 1894

DATE OF CRIME: June 13, 1894

CRIMINAL ARRESTED: YES

DESCRIPTION OF CRIME: On the morning of June 13, the suspect stole a horse to travel to the center of London, where he committed fraud by passing off fake currency to a storekeeper. When the storekeeper realized his mistake, he called the police, after which the suspect fled, evading arrest down a back alley. He then vandalized an image of our Queen and attempted to murder the pursuing officer. While he escaped initially, it was his previous crimes that gave him away and we arrested him today. He had committed all but one of these crimes beforehand and they were on his record. He will not be getting out for some time.

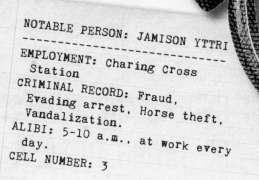

NOTABLE PERSON: JAMISON YTTRI

EMPLOYMENT: Charing Cross
   Station
CRIMINAL RECORD: Fraud,
   Evading arrest, Horse theft,
   Vandalization.
ALIBI: 5-10 a.m., at work every
   day.
CELL NUMBER: 3

NOTABLE PERSON: DUNCAN GREAVES

EMPLOYMENT: Store Assistant, Hart Street.
CRIMINAL RECORD: Theft, Vandalization.
ALIBI: 12-8 p.m., at work every day.
CELL NUMBER: 5

The sheer amount of information provided in the folder was perplexing. Holmes was already shaking his head.

"Watson, I would like you to deduce the prime suspect in this case."

"The prime suspect?"

"Let me put it another way: the only suspect remaining, given all of the information contained within this room. Certain things will eliminate people from the notable persons list provided on these cards. When you can see no other option but one, for many different reasons, the conclusion you come to will be the only logical one."

"Then I should begin."

"Begin? My dear Watson, I had hoped you were nearly done."

I took a deep breath. Holmes's skills had no doubt returned to him, yet perhaps his lack of confidence in his state of mind required me to confirm what he seemingly already knew.

When I had only one suspect left, I knew I could proceed.

HINTS
Difficult, turn to page 184
Medium, turn to page 188
Easy, turn to page 195
For solutions, turn to page 215

"YOU MUST UNDERSTAND THAT COMING HERE AND TRYING TO SOLVE THE CASE EXONERATES HIM."

It could not be so. Holmes's mental state after his near-death experience had left him confused and unlike himself, but for him to be responsible for the murder seemed entirely ridiculous.

"The way you are looking at me suggests that you have come to the same conclusion as I have."

"You? You are the killer?"

"That is the same result we came to," announced Lestrade, who was standing by the entrance.

"You must understand that coming here and trying to solve the case exonerates him," I pleaded.

"The evidence is the evidence, Dr. Watson," Lestrade insisted. "So . . ."

"So, he must observe protocol, Watson," Holmes acknowledged. "Our actions in this room do not clear me, yet do give him comfort that all may not be what it seems."

"I'm afraid I shall have to arrest the two of you."

"Both of us?"

"You two have such a close relationship that it is only prudent of me to take precautions. In the meantime, is there anything I can do for you? Anyone to inform?"

"There is little point, Lestrade," Holmes stated confidently, smiling as he volunteered his freedom.

I could not believe the relaxed attitude of my friend. Lestrade nodded down the corridor, indicating where we were to follow him, and two more officers entered, standing beside him to avoid risking of our flight. Holmes waltzed ahead, making turn after turn through the station, confident in exactly where he was heading.

"Cell five, is it, Lestrade?"

"How did you?"

"And I assume we are to be contained together?"

"Yes, but . . ."

"This way, Watson," he boomed.

While I was in shock, and reeling at the thought of what was to happen next, Holmes was content.

Can you, dear reader, deduce how Holmes knew where we were to be held?

Holmes had recalled the chief superintendent announcing that the cells were full, yet one of the prisoners was to be let go. No doubt expecting our visit to the police station to end this way, he had deduced the cell that the prisoner had been held in from the notable person cards.

We were surprisingly gently ushered into the room, which was of a size big enough to hold multiple occupants.

"Why are you so calm about all of this, Holmes?"

"Because one of two things will happen next. Either I will be convicted for a crime I do not believe that I committed, or I will be released, and I have little control over which way the proverbial coin will fall."

So, for now, we waited.

"Either I will be convicted for a crime I do not believe that I committed, or I will be released."

CHAPTER EIGHT

THE CELLS

I was calmer than I would have expected to be, finding myself in such a position. Of course, I was sure that *I* was not responsible for a murder. And besides, my experience both of Holmes and of the criminal justice system was surprisingly positive. I had noticed that they each had a propensity to succeed, sometimes against all odds. However, the length of time we would be in this cell was not up to us. It was beyond our control, unless we could find some ingenious method of escape, which I doubted.

Scouting around our environment was a matter of habit now. Two beds sat in the far corners of the room, a table was next to one with a Bible on it and an oil lantern for lighting. Setting fire to the mattress was probably the only damage that we could do with the lantern, but I was still surprised to see that it was there at all. Perhaps the lack of natural light—beyond that which came from a tiny barred window high up on one of the walls—made it a necessity.

It suddenly struck me that the process of deduction that Holmes was such an expert in—and I was learning to improve on—was just one half of the story of the cogs of justice. Once our crimes were solved and the perpetrators incarcerated, this was where they would continue their lives. It was certainly something to think about. My friend had not said a word for a while, and the silence around us was painful. How would a prisoner occupy their time? Just thinking? But of what? Their crimes? Would they find apologetic redemption, or fall into a seething longing for retribution toward whomever had caused their current situation?

The silence was broken by a ratcheting sound coming from the bars we had been led through. Holmes was turning a crank. Was this going to achieve something that he thought might free us? Surely, it would be utterly ridiculous for a jail to contain such a feature.

EROS

OUT

"Exercise," Holmes blurted out, having noticed my interest in his actions.

"Excuse me?"

"This crank. It is connected through some cogs to flaps on the other side, probably sat in a container of sand to make it difficult to move."

"What does it do?"

"Nothing. That is the point. It is a meaningless action that serves to tire the occupant and give them some physical activity."

"Quite peculiar," I noted.

"Indeed. Guards may require we perform a certain amount of it every day to earn meals. It instigates subservience and obedience."

Was this to be our lives for the foreseeable future? The reality of our situation was beginning to hit me, just as my calm demeanor was swiftly leaving me. My thoughts were interrupted by hushed words and a shadow down the corridor, moving away. Looking over at the wall outside our cell, I saw scrawling on the wall. Many of the bricks had letters written on them, as well as a strange design with four symbols around it.

The light seemed to flicker, and a tall, albeit slightly hunched, man wearing a black, billowing robe over an expensive suit and a teal-blue necktie glided across the floor.

"Mr. Sherlock Holmes, Dr. John Watson," he announced. Holmes smiled, a glint in his eyes revealing his anticipation of something surprising.

"You have us at a disadvantage, sir," Holmes probed.

"You may call me Parkinson," the man replied.

"For someone to get in here, manage to have the guards leave at his whim, and smuggle something in must infer power of some kind."

Parkinson smiled and pulled a hand out from behind him, revealing a pristine well-decorated cake with thirteen candles set on it. "Happy birthday," he announced.

"Whose birthday is it?" I asked.

"Does it matter?"

"I suppose not. Thank you, good sir," Holmes said, reaching out and taking the cake from him.

"His posture," Holmes muttered, confirming to me how he had known.

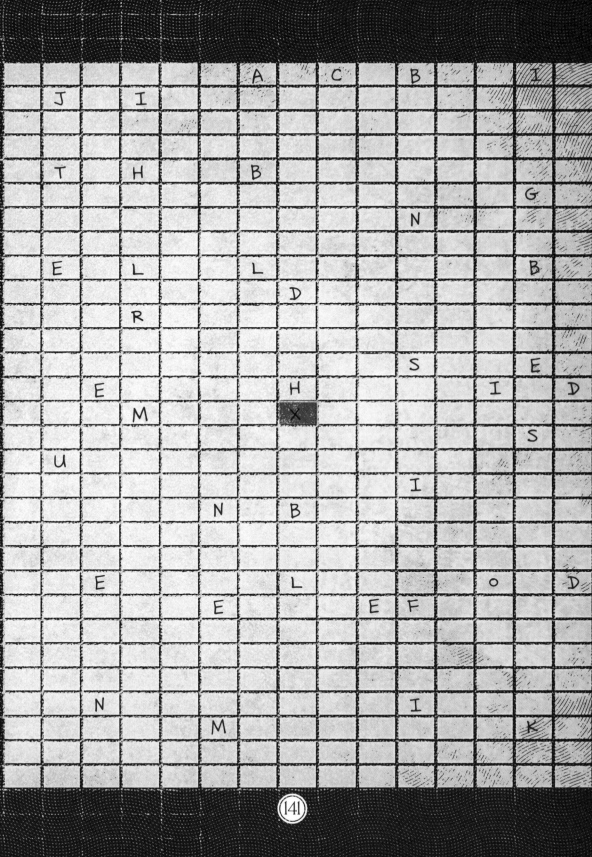

The man turned to depart, but I could not allow him to leave without at least answering some questions. "Wait, who are you?"

"I was wondering if you even cared."

"Don't tell me," Holmes began. "A powerful secret organization. You scratch our backs and we'll scratch yours?"

"We are not so secretive. Powerful, however, is accurate. I represent the Wexell fellowship. We have always been around, in one way or another. Despite our considerable foresight and power, from time to time we are . . . shall we say . . . outmaneuvered."

"We will not simply agree to assist you," Holmes said, with a chuckle.

"You will because, believe it or not, our objectives are aligned."

"What objectives?" Holmes persisted. I took a step back to better observe.

"Ours are neither nefarious nor suspect."

"According to you."

"We are not behind what is happening to you, Mr. Holmes."

"And yet you are privy to the information about it."

"We recruit the very best and try to give them the creative freedoms required to advance society."

"I'm not interested in a job."

"Oh, we're not here for you, Mr. Holmes. We are here because of you. The freedom we offer can sometimes be misused by someone with enough foresight of their own, and it seems like the plan set in motion when you were in Reichenbach can only have been designed by one person."

"Moriarty."

"Indeed. I am ashamed to say that he was once a part of our organization. He fooled us for a long time, gaining power and influence in our circles, until it became clear that he was using the knowledge we gave him access to

for . . . less than altruistic purposes."

"And that is what you are, is it? Altruistic?"

"As far as it is possible to be. All actions have good and bad consequences on a microlevel. The ends justify the means would be the most appropriate idiom, I suspect."

"Then you believe that Moriarty organized all of this in case of his death."

"And this will end badly for both you and us if it goes his way. Your escape from this cell serves us both."

"Then it is a pleasure to be working together."

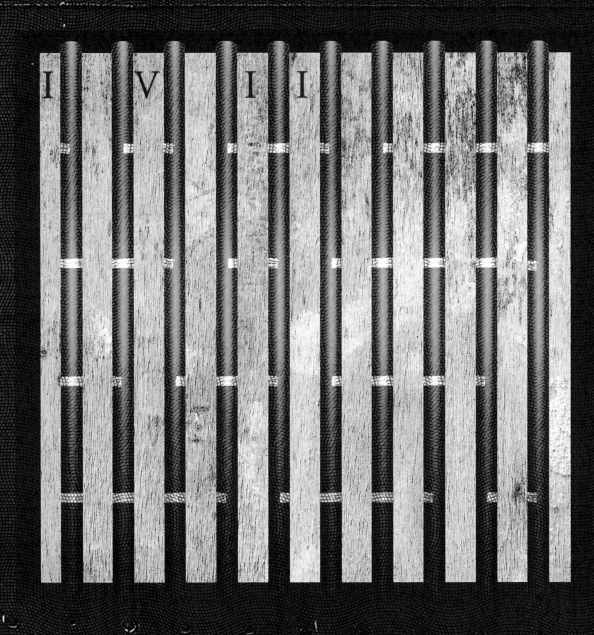

Parkinson nodded and turned around to take his leave. Holmes and I stayed silent as he wandered over to the brick wall and raised his hand, tapping directly on the one red brick marked with an "X" in the center. Why was that important?

"Oh, and assuming you succeed in securing your escape, speak to the Cyphstress at the Circus of New Orleans, which is taking residence in London for the next few weeks. Your skills will probably get more out of her than we were able to."

And, with that, the man returned to the shadows.

"That cake is not for eating, is it, Holmes?" I questioned, somewhat rhetorically. He merely smiled. "Well then, we'd better take a closer look at our surroundings."

There was little left in the room still unexplored, but standing back from the discussion had led me to a further discovery about our place of containment. The bars of our cell had some white paint over some of them. I examined them for a while but came up short.

"Perhaps that is not a method of encoding information, Watson, but merely something to tell us how to split other information that we may find later."

"I do not understand, Holmes."

"Look at how many white lines there are. Perhaps if we have some information of that length, it will become clearer."

I shifted my gaze over to the remaining items in the room: our two beds. Looking back up at Holmes, we both understood what to do, and each headed to the closest one. I picked up the thin, dirty mattress, if it could even be called such a thing, and looked on the underside. While I could find nothing there, I noticed a small slit in the side of it, and perhaps foolishly reached straight in. I drew back in pain, having touched something sharp. Not one to be defeated, I cautiously reintroduced my hand to the gap and found the culprit: a shard of what seemed like a mirror. In a corner was the remnants of what I assumed was a brand name: "Harvey." I clung to it, unsure for now of why I had it but hoping it would be useful for its reflective purposes instead of being used as a tool of destruction.

Holmes had also been successful, although not by looking inside his mattress but instead by moving it. He had exposed a square grid on the wooden base and a single die. The grid had letters throughout it, as well as numbers in the top right-hand corners.

"Do you know what this is, Watson?" Holmes exclaimed.

"Other than the obvious, no."

"This grid is intended to have the die roll around it. You start on the highlighted square, with the number written in the top corner facing up,

and must roll the die either up, right, down, or left to cover every square in the grid once; the only caveat being that the route must show the numbers on the top of the die when you land on them. There should be only one way of 'rolling the grid.'"

Somehow, I could see that everything in this place had been designed to give us a chance at getting out, yet I could see no other way of escaping but the way we came in: the huge iron gate, which the guard had locked with a key. I was sure that the guard did not have the only key; I knew I needed to find another. I took a deep breath. My friend was still working things out, but evidently it would be some time before he would be fully capable, so I knew I would have to find the key myself.

When I had discovered where it was, I knew I could proceed.

HINTS
Difficult, turn to page 184
Medium, turn to page 189
Easy, turn to page 195
For solutions, turn to page 218

S^6	$-^5$	H^1	R^2	S^1	D^3	F^2	D^4
O^4	R^5	A^4	A^3	$-^3$	D^1	D^2	D^1
R^1	V^6	$-^6$	B^5	C^6	D^1	K^4	K^3
E^3	E^2	Y^4	N^2	A^4	D^5	K^4	K^6
$-^6$	T^5	L^3	D^1	D^1	D^5	D^6 END	D^4
A^6	R^4	E^5	D^2	K^3	D^3	D^2	D^1
T^2	$-^6$	S^4	D^6	D^1	K^2	F^3	F^1
S^1	X^2	$:^4$	K^5	D^4	D^2	D^3	K^5

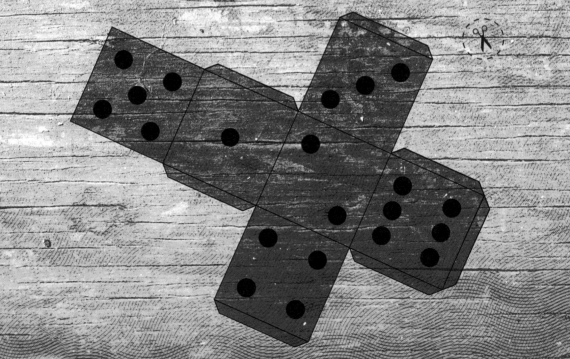

"I slid the key into the lock and turned it with a satisfying click. It creaked open and we hastily took our leave."

The key was in the Bible. An obvious hiding place, yet one in which I would probably not have looked anytime soon. The Wexell fellowship must have planned this all in advance, right down to the delivery of the cake. But why not just give us the key? Of course. This was a test, specifically designed for us, knowing that we would both be extremely unlikely to look in the Bible before solving the conundrums and complications around the room. We had passed. This Wexell fellowship must be watching to know that we had not simply fortuitously stumbled upon the correct pages in the Bible; after all, there was not a lot to explore in here. I could not shake the feeling that it was a test of Holmes's state of mind itself. Either way, we now had a means of escape and had to take it.

I slid the key into the lock and turned it with a satisfying click. It creaked open and we hastily took our leave. The area was remarkably silent, perhaps due to Parkinson's influence, yet at the end of the hallway leading to the main entrance to the station two officers were discussing something.

"We must not be discovered. This is certainly our only chance," Holmes insisted, confirming what I myself had surmised.

"Then we should await their departure," I suggested.

Holmes nodded and we paused just around the corner. I stuck my head

back around it briefly to see that they were still there, locked in conversation.

"My dear friend," Holmes began, "we may be at the end of our journey with the slightest wrong move here."

"Then we will have to be sure that we make the right move."

"Indeed. We have no means of disguise other than our demeanors."

"So, what do you suggest we do?"

"One must remain entirely convincing to pass anyone we see. If someone sees you, it is imperative that you appear as if you are meant to be here and, more important, that you don't appear to be afraid of them seeing you."

"I understand."

"Remain calm, smile at anyone that looks at you, and keep moving. It may help if we instigate a conversation, more banal than the situation demands, to sell the illusion."

"I see. And when we make the decision to move, we should not turn back; it would arouse suspicion, I imagine," I suggested.

"Correct."

Nervously, I poked my head around the corner and walked straight into the path of an oncoming officer who was turning the corner. My demeanor fell instantly, Holmes's words useless to me in a moment of panic. The officer spoke first.

"Sorry, sir, excuse me," he said warmly.

THE CELLS

Stepping to the side, he paced onward and into a small office not far away. It seemed like this would be easier than we thought, given that not everyone in the building knew we were now fugitives.

"Come on then, Watson," Holmes announced, charging around the corner. I quickly followed and wondered what to make our "innocuous" conversation about.

"The weather has been particularly awful this season, has it not?" I started.

"The weather? The weather is your banal conversation topic, Watson?"

"Well, it's not like I had a lot of time to think."

"Of course, recognizing Roman numerals, specific heights of candles, and dice rolling is a trifling matter, but the weather is the best you can come up with."

We reached the main reception area and kept up our pace. "So, what would you have suggested instead?" I asked, considerably more upset than I should have been at the insinuation of my weakness in attempting to go unnoticed. "A pet perhaps. A dog that was getting sick?"

"An ill animal? How is that in any way better?"

"Isn't it obvious?"

"No, it isn't."

Stepping out of the station, I wanted to stop to enjoy our success, but I realized we needed to keep going despite being out of immediate danger.

"Excellent work, Watson," Holmes offered.

"Excuse me?"

"You were superb."

"I thought you said the weather was a terrible conversation topic."

"Oh, Watson. It was never about the topic. It was about seeming sincere and authentic, and it genuinely felt like you were arguing with me about something. That's all it took to seem like we were not hiding anything."

"Well, then I suppose we both did rather well," I confirmed.

"No time for congratulations, Watson. We're off

to the Circus of New Orleans."

We hailed a taxicab as soon as we could and were on our way.

The Circus of New Orleans was currently stationed in London's Hampstead Heath, fresh from the exotic and mysterious Louisiana—or at least that is what it purported. A huge wooden structure with magnificent red drapes floating to the ground almost shouted its name in announcing its presence to the dark surroundings, with the Heath being as close to rural in London as it was possible to be. Despite the lavish, exciting entrance, from which the soft glow of lights inside warmed the gradually darkening natural light of the evening, there were no guests. The circus was yet to open; perhaps the wonders inside were still being set up.

After the entrance came the enormous tent. Posters along the walkway announced some of the feats to be witnessed, including one that caught my eye: "The Cyphstress and her voodoo enchantments."

Sherlock Holmes and I could not have known what we were walking into, but at least we knew now that we

GREATEST SHOW ON EARTH

THE

Circus

OF

NEW ORLEANS

BUY TICKETS NOW

were in the right place. We approached the entrance and Holmes looked over at me.

"After you, my good friend," he offered.

I hesitated. My trepidation at the unknown made me question Holmes's motives in allowing me to go first. He raised his eyebrows expectantly.

"How kind," I replied, and pushed the flaps aside, before marching in.

CHAPTER NINE

THE CIRCUS

I emerged through the curtains to an extravagant and flamboyant sight: the spacious circle of the arena opened up before me, with carnival games arranged around the outside, and a center stage with seating on it. A small area at the back, covered over by red and yellow tarpaulin, served as an entrance to the stage. A decisive lack of sound suggested that the place was deserted.

Posters of some of the acts and attractions were stuck haphazardly around the arena.

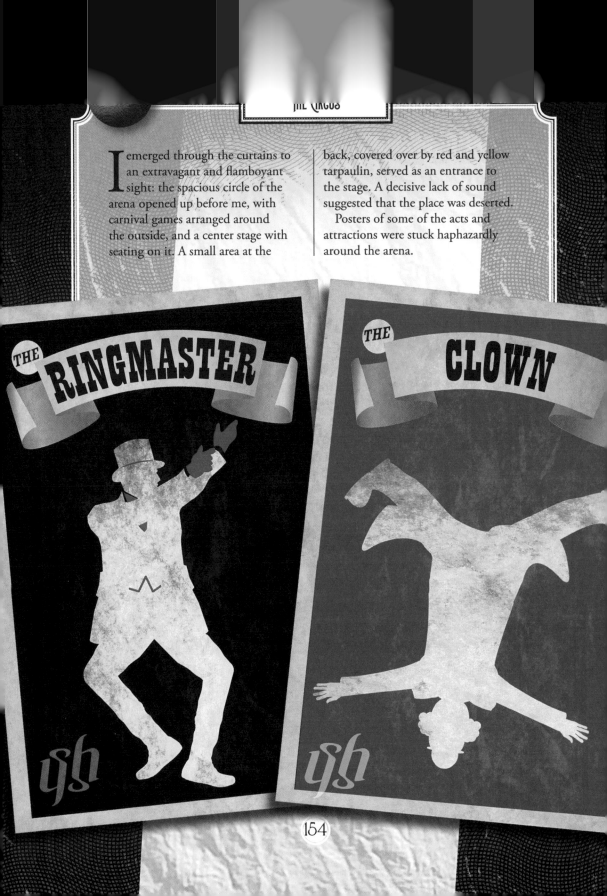

THE RINGMASTER

THE CLOWN

THE **STRONGMAN**

THE **JUGGLER**

"A DECISIVE LACK OF SOUND SUGGESTED THAT THE PLACE WAS DESERTED."

The nearest stall to the entrance showed four differently tinted vertical glass tubes with numbers and lines marked on the side of each of them. One of them had a ball in it, exactly the size of the gap between the lines. A funnel at the top of each one revealed the purpose of the game. It was a simple case of trying to aim correctly. Perhaps one would win a prize if enough balls were successfully landed.

The silence was broken by Holmes's voice. "Hello? Is anybody here?" he boomed.

I instinctively tried to silence him, as if our presence here was forbidden. Indeed, we shouldn't be here, but Holmes's confidence would probably be useful if we were caught.

A female voice wafted around the auditorium: "Mr. Holmes, Dr. Watson, come to the tent with the purple trim."

Holmes smiled at me and raised an eyebrow, clearly proud of his decision to call out. My disapproval must have been plastered across my face, which only served to make him smile more. Nonetheless, we began walking toward the tent in question. Holmes gestured for me to peer in first, while my nerves were heightened by a simple question. How did whoever called out to us know us by name?

I looked inside and was greeted with what I assumed was a close approximation to explain how they knew: it was a fortune-teller.

"Dr. Watson, it is a pleasure to finally meet you," the teller called out with a soft southern American accent. "And what brings you to me this evening?"

"I assumed that since you knew my name, you would know my business."

"A simple parlor trick, I'm afraid," Holmes blurted out, much to the teller's disdain.

"I am the Cyphstress, and my powers, although limited at present, are *very* far from a trick, Mr. Holmes."

"Then how, pray tell, do you do it?" he provoked.

"Communing with the spirits has its benefits, and its dangers."

"Madame, please dispense with the frivolity. If you have information for us, then you simply must tell us."

"Instead, I have a gift for you."

She reached over her table, which was covered in a rich, purple velvet, and placed a single silver token on top of a spread of tarot cards.

"Are we not supposed to cross *your* palm with silver?" Holmes quipped.

The Cyphstress remained smiling, although it was clearly an effort. "I cannot tell you more. His spies are everywhere. But follow the silver, and you will have your answer."

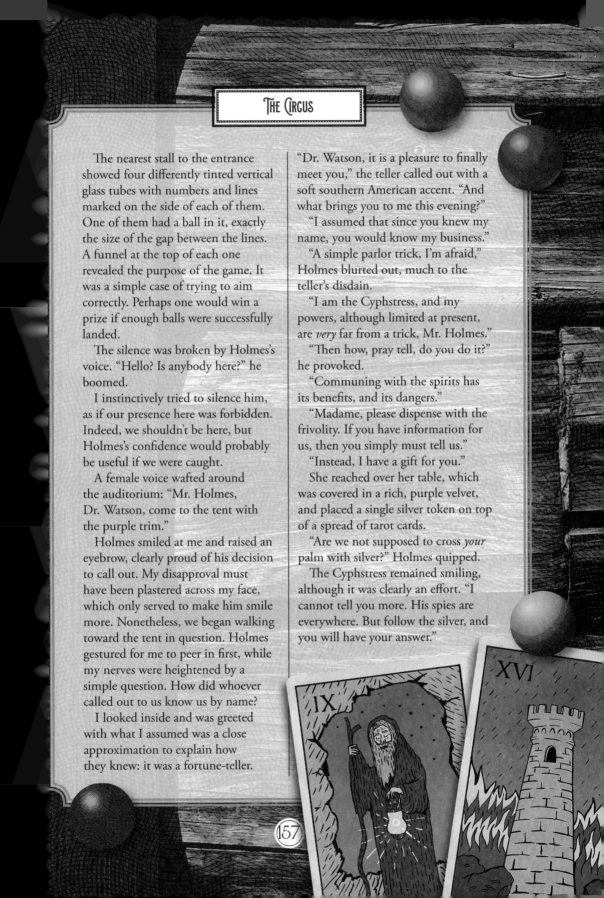

"How terribly specific," Holmes drawled, before taking his leave. I nodded to the Cyphstress, picked up the silver coin, and started following Holmes out.

"Dr. Watson. While I have you on your own, there is something I must tell you," the Cyphstress murmured.

"What is it?" I replied, intrigued as to why Holmes was excluded.

"Death is coming."

"Excuse me?"

"My cards are guidance, but Death is clear."

"To whom? And why are you telling me alone?"

"Because this is Sherlock Holmes's reading. Death will come to him."

I stepped back, a little startled. Surely this could not be the truth—-merely speculation and the aforementioned parlor tricks designed to instill fear and suspicion. Either way, it had shaken me. As I backed out of the curtain and into the large main arena, I looked over at Holmes—already investigating his next find—and could only hope that the reading was incorrect. "Over here, Watson," he called out.

Holmes was looking at a pile of six metallic panels with grooves and markings cut neatly into them and a frame built in the shape of a cube. Above it was a sign: "The Bewilder Box." The panels clearly fit together onto the frame, but how?

THE MOON

THE SUN

EMPRESS

THE WORLD

JUSTICE

LOVERS

STRENGTH

DEATH

"Holmes looked up and swayed to the side, staggering into the nearest wall."

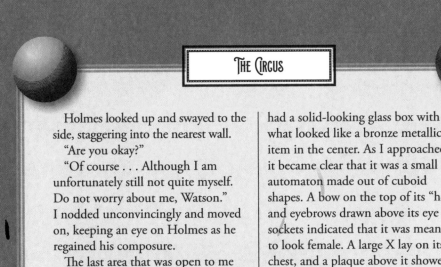

Holmes looked up and swayed to the side, staggering into the nearest wall.

"Are you okay?"

"Of course . . . Although I am unfortunately still not quite myself. Do not worry about me, Watson." I nodded unconvincingly and moved on, keeping an eye on Holmes as he regained his composure.

The last area that was open to me had a solid-looking glass box with what looked like a bronze metallic item in the center. As I approached, it became clear that it was a small automaton made out of cuboid shapes. A bow on the top of its "head" and eyebrows drawn above its eye sockets indicated that it was meant to look female. A large X lay on its chest, and a plaque above it showed its name: Xellda.

Suspiciously, I approached, worried that some mechanism would spring it to life in order to shock my attention toward it, yet it remained motionless. I followed its gaze down to a slot in the side and it dawned on me that my silver token would fit into it perfectly.

"Holmes, take a look at this."

"That is some construction," he commented, approaching. "And I sense that you wish to activate it?"

"Why else were we given this coin?"

My friend smiled at me, clearly excited at having a starting point, and nodded toward Xellda, encouraging me to use the silver, which I, of course, did. The token slipped in perfectly and, after a couple of seconds, the automaton came to life, moving erratically until it seemed

6453 THE LONDON COFFEE HOUSE **6453**

6534 ALHAMBRA, LEICESTER SQUARE **6534**

to settle, facing us directly. A blast of steam erupted from what looked like its ears, and the whoosh of sound settled into a tone, like a musical instrument. As the mechanisms shifted, it made different notes that clearly sounded like words. It was speaking to us.

"Some try to delay, some try to cheat, but in the end, we always will meet. Evil does hate me, I sing moral song, my scales breed satisfaction, against those who've done wrong.

I can be of conviction, or muscles or will, my power is used both, to save and to kill. You're all around me, yet without me you'd die, your resourceful sphere, is where you all lie.

"This precise order is important. Disregard all others."

With that, Xellda collapsed into her initial state, having given us what we needed. Holmes and I looked at each other, surprised at what had just

4365 ROYAL STRAND THEATER **4365**

5436 THE ARMY AND NAVY CLUB **5436**

5643 THE ALBERY **5643**

6345 ADELPHI THEATER **6345**

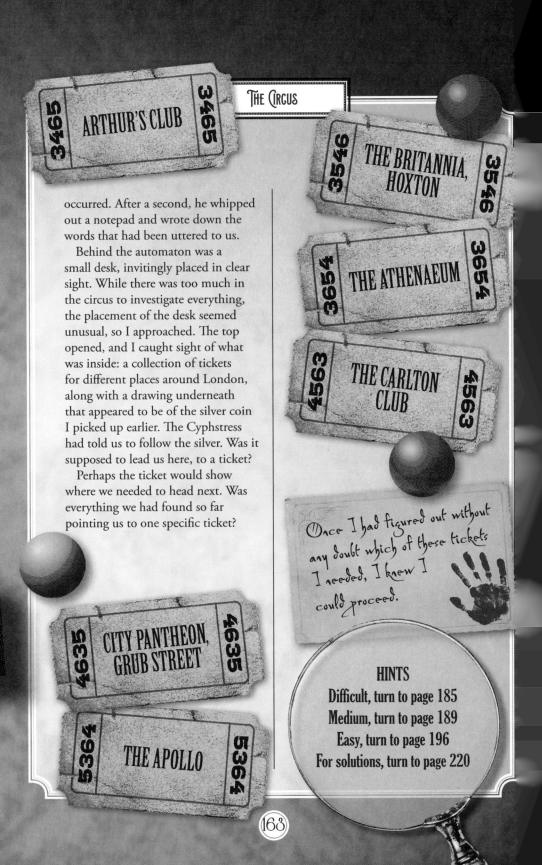

ARTHUR'S CLUB — 3465

THE BRITANNIA, HOXTON — 3546

THE ATHENAEUM — 3654

THE CARLTON CLUB — 4563

CITY PANTHEON, GRUB STREET — 4635

THE APOLLO — 5364

occurred. After a second, he whipped out a notepad and wrote down the words that had been uttered to us.

Behind the automaton was a small desk, invitingly placed in clear sight. While there was too much in the circus to investigate everything, the placement of the desk seemed unusual, so I approached. The top opened, and I caught sight of what was inside: a collection of tickets for different places around London, along with a drawing underneath that appeared to be of the silver coin I picked up earlier. The Cyphstress had told us to follow the silver. Was it supposed to lead us here, to a ticket?

Perhaps the ticket would show where we needed to head next. Was everything we had found so far pointing us to one specific ticket?

Once I had figured out without any doubt which of these tickets I needed, I knew I could proceed.

HINTS
Difficult, turn to page 185
Medium, turn to page 189
Easy, turn to page 196
For solutions, turn to page 220

A ticket to the theater—and to one of London's grandest.

I was certain that this was where everything that we had experienced over the past two days was leading us, and that it would give up the secrets we both desired and deserved. "Excellent work, Watson," Holmes smiled, no doubt proud of my work in his metaphorical absence.

"Thank you," I returned.

"I assume our card-reading friend in the tent spoke further to you about me?"

"How did you . . . ?"

"The time you took. It was obvious you and she had more to say, and for her to wait until I was gone meant that it was, in all likelihood, about me."

"Quite right, my friend," I admitted. "Although I am unsure of its relevance."

"Did she claim I was going to die?"

"Something like that."

"Well, it's a good job neither of us believe in that kind of poppycock then, isn't it?"

"Indeed."

While I knew she couldn't be right, the words "Death is coming" were striking enough to make me doubt

STAGE

myself. Perhaps Holmes should not accompany me to the theater. Perhaps not accompanying me would lead to death. With no way of knowing, I did not put up a fuss, opting to see what would happen instead of worrying about the possibilities.

"Come on, Watson. We can't keep Death waiting."

Sherlock Holmes had a bounce in his step that I hadn't seen since before his injury, like he was thrilled at the prospect of proving someone wrong. I followed him out, glancing back at the purple tent as I passed. The curtains were open, yet the Cyphstress was nowhere to be seen.

We left the large tent to the darkness of the night and picked up a carriage into the heart of London. The driver took us to the entrance of the theater, adorned with a huge sign for a new show: "The Detective's End—Opening Soon." I noted that the first date of the run was tomorrow. How poignant.

Of course this was where whoever was behind this would have chosen to end the tale. The doors were open and Holmes stormed in, eager to come face to face with our antagonist. We were clearly at the end game now.

DOOR

CHAPTER TEN

THE THEATER

The lobby of the theater appeared, at first glance, to be grander than anywhere else we had visited on our journey so far. Quite how much of it was real and how much was simply cheap ornamentation was anyone's guess—although I was sure Holmes had some thoughts, if I cared to trouble him—but we paced forward together with no fear, heading toward the double doors that led to the seats. Our movement, however, was halted by a lock.

We could not continue. Looking around, posters and banners remained in place advertising the acts for the last show that had appeared there: Harry Houdini, wowing audiences with a spectacle that would certainly go over Holmes's head. In fact, I was certain he would hate it.

"I do adore the magic of the theater, Watson," Holmes announced, much to my surprise.

"But the trickery . . . Surely it would not fool you, Holmes?" I replied.

"A stage magician is much the same as a crime scene, or a person to read, my dear friend. It is a puzzle to be solved, one that has been specifically put in place to confuse an everyday audience."

"Is the enjoyment not in being fooled?"

"I spend my days untangling riddles, Watson. Why would I want to be fooled?"

Holmes paced off to the side of the lobby, looking for other openings from which to enter the main area and view the stage in its inevitable splendor. He could find none, but a door tucked into a corner—adorned with a sign that read "Employees Only"—opened easily enough. Unusually, he held it open for me.

"Why, thank you, Holmes," I acknowledged, half wondering whether he meant for me to blunder into any danger before him. A small, dimly lit corridor presented itself, instantly dropping the facade of opulence. The public side required money to be spent on it, whereas I could have sworn I had seen a rat crawling away from us as we proceeded onward.

The hallway ended at a doorway to a dressing room and entering it was inevitable, because we had no other choices available. The room was small and remarkably full. Houdini's run of shows had only just ended, and he must not have taken everything away with him as yet.

A rack was in one corner, laden with costumes for various parts in his spectacle. I picked one up and was shocked at its luxuriousness. There were hidden pockets and crevices all over it, probably to help with the mystery of the acts. Next to the rack was a set list that described what was needed, and when. None of it, however, seemed particularly worth wasting any more time on.

VICTORIA
AND THE
BUTLER

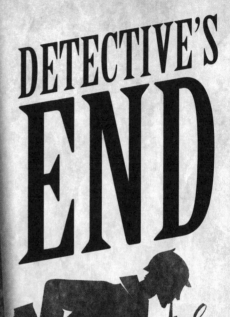

DETECTIVE'S
END

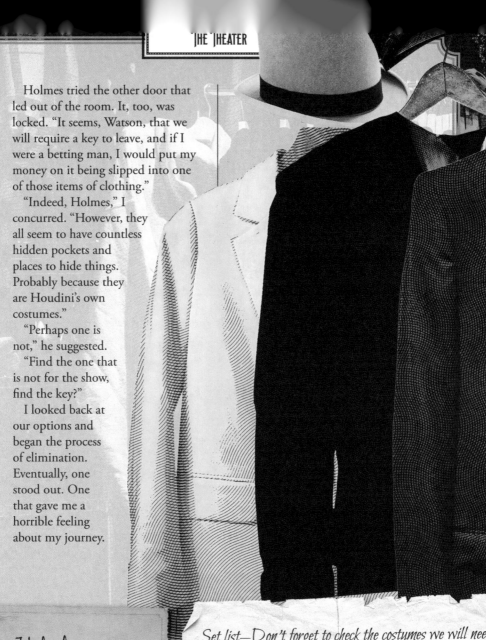

Holmes tried the other door that led out of the room. It, too, was locked. "It seems, Watson, that we will require a key to leave, and if I were a betting man, I would put my money on it being slipped into one of those items of clothing."

"Indeed, Holmes," I concurred. "However, they all seem to have countless hidden pockets and places to hide things. Probably because they are Houdini's own costumes."

"Perhaps one is not," he suggested.

"Find the one that is not for the show, find the key?"

I looked back at our options and began the process of elimination. Eventually, one stood out. One that gave me a horrible feeling about my journey.

When I had only one costume left, I knew I could proceed.

Set list—Don't forget to check the costumes we will need:
Introduction—Smart with bow tie and top hat
Act 1 (including stocks/ animal extravaganza)
Need assistant in red dress for the coffin trick
Act 2 (including water escape and workshop effect)
Finale—Inverted colors from introduction

The train ticket collector's uniform did not seem to fit in with the show as described by the set list or the posters on the wall. It had to be something else. I slipped my hand into a few pockets until I hit something metallic: the key.

Proudly, but also tentatively, I held it up and approached the door. "This is it, Holmes," I whispered. "The end of our journey."

"Perhaps, dear friend. Would you care to take the lead? It has been mostly your work that has got us here."

"Awfully kind of you. Unless, of course, you are expecting me to come face to face with danger first?"

"Who knows, Watson?" He wondered, with a smirk. I used the key and flung the door open, hoping to catch anyone lurking there off guard, but instead I was simply faced with an empty hallway, dark and dusty. Almost immediately, I realized that we were standing in the wings of the main stage.

Something caught Holmes's eye and he rushed ahead, straight into the center of the stage, where a small item sat. I looked around the rafters and noted elaborate props and items hanging suspended, no doubt waiting to be lowered for the spectacle of the audience.

Turning back to Holmes, I saw it was a hat. What is more, a hat that I recognized, and Holmes had bent down to pick it up. A jarring snapping sound echoed around the auditorium, and we both looked up—alas, too late.

My heart beat faster as I watched an enormous glass chamber fall from the ceiling above us. It fell around Holmes even as he stood up, trapping him inside a contraption that had clearly been borrowed from Houdini's show. Was this the famous water escape that I had heard so much about?

Holmes kept his calm remarkably well, gently probing the glass panels for a sign of weakness. He found none. Meanwhile, I looked around for some tool to assist in his release, before I was interrupted by a deep voice gently rolling down the auditorium. Searching, I lit upon a figure up in the dress circle, silhouetted by a large spotlight that was now pointing down on the glass cubicle.

"Mr. Holmes. Dr. Watson. I am truly humbled by your presence," the figure called out. "I assume you recognize me?"

Holmes cried out, but the glass muted his voice. The man stepped directly in front of the light and, as he further blocked it, I could see his details more clearly. I also spotted a limp as he moved. He was right, I had indeed seen him before—he was the ticket collector from my train to Cookham. What was he doing here?

The significance of his uniform being in the dressing room was now confirmed to me, but I was still confused. I glanced over at Holmes, who was now increasingly frantic and calling out almost undecipherable words to me. It sounded like he was asking "Who had joined the party?"

The ticket collector gestured down toward Holmes. "Thank you for bringing him to me, Dr. Watson. I could not have found him myself."

"I don't understand. Are you behind this whole thing? The attempts on Holmes's life?"

"Of course. Was there ever any doubt?" Things still did not make sense. I looked over at Holmes and the hat that he had picked up. Where did I recognize the hat from? Of course. It had fallen down the Reichenbach Falls.

"For the party!" Holmes screamed once more.

"What party?" I replied. He shook his head. Perhaps I was misinterpreting the sound of his words? What else did they sound like?

The figure laughed. "He is warning you about me, Dr. Watson."

The truth dawned on me. This was a man I had never seen the face of before my recent experience on the train. But he was a man I had known from afar for a long time. A man who was even now looking to gain an advantage against the only person who had ever challenged him. Not "for the party . . ." This was Professor James Moriarty. Holmes had been trying to tell me.

"How did you survive the Falls?" I called out. He was supposed to be dead; Death had indeed come for us.

"The same way your friend did. Fortuity. Mr. Holmes must have sustained greater injuries than I, and as such is not yet working on full steam."

"He knew that someone was after him."

"And involved you to try to help him discover whom. Instead, you merely led him directly to me. His final chance was to avoid the trap I had laid for him, and yet there he is, inside Houdini's greatest escape."

"Why not just kill him, or me?"

"Until you found Holmes for me, I could not have found him. That is why I set up all of this, to convince you both to reveal yourselves to me. It was my final opportunity to take advantage of Holmes's injuries and dull senses."

"But they found your body. You were dead."

"Alas, Dr. Watson, they did not. I searched far and wide for someone that fit my own appearance. My contacts within St. Mary's were very forthcoming, and even told me which body to dig up. I believe you know him as Butcher, or perhaps McAvoy. Then a wigmaker helped change my appearance and the most convincing illusion of my disappearance was complete. Far better than my ex-colleague Harry Houdini could achieve."

"What do you plan to do with us now?"

"The pleasure of the conflict for both Mr. Holmes and me is in the uncertainty. The opportunity for both sides to succeed. Do not doubt my ruthless nature, of course. This setup is my way of stacking the odds undoubtedly in my favor. But mark my words, Doctor, you have a chance, albeit a slim one, and that glimmer of hope will lead you to attempt to save your friend. That is when I will make my escape and, when you fail, I will be unchallenged in everything I attempt in future."

Moriarty sneered while I took a second to think before replying. This time was long enough for him to pull on a rope, causing water to begin streaming into Holmes's container. His shoes were submerged even as I looked around for an item to smash the glass.

"I have removed all items that you could use to free him with brute force, Doctor."

What should I do? Before I could act at all, Moriarty stepped away from the light and moved toward the upper exit. "Have an enjoyable party, you two," he shouted, before disappearing from view.

I had to save Holmes before he drowned in this contraption. Time was running out, but I needed to regain my composure and work out what this slim chance of victory was that Moriarty said he had left. I looked up above the stage. More items were hanging, certainly items for Houdini's show. Which of them could I lower without risking further calamity? At this point, I did not know. Across the stage, I saw a number of ropes which were marked with letters from A to H.

Holmes was now pointing frantically at the floor. Looking underneath his cage, it was clear what he had seen: a trapdoor. If I could find a way to release it, he would fall through the stage, and the water would be released, too.

I rushed over to the ropes and noticed a large lever marked "Trapdoors." That must be the one, yet a thin metal pipe was holding it in place—protected by a small lock with three digits. Examining it more closely, the pipe was delicate and hollow but even so I could not bend it or wrench it out of the way to pull the lever. As Moriarty said, brute force was not an option. But now I knew that was what I needed to do to save Holmes. I could try guessing the numbers, but I would have no certainty that I could complete the process in time.

I noticed that the back of the stage curtains had a curious set of eight knot designs on one side, while on the other a series of animal silhouettes were sewn into the fabric. Both sides had lines crisscrossing to the edge of the curtain, but which ended there.

Holmes tapped his glass. I read his lips speaking what could only be: "In your own time." Suddenly, he saw something on the opposite side of the glass. I approached and was able to hear what he was saying.

"Watson, listen to me. I can see some shapes. Three sets of six dots. Some of the dots are empty holes and some of them have black pins in them. Each set of six dots is in the same pattern. Two columns and three rows. The first set has

176

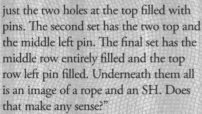

just the two holes at the top filled with pins. The second set has the two top and the middle left pin. The final set has the middle row entirely filled and the top row left pin filled. Underneath them all is an image of a rope and an SH. Does that make any sense?"

"I do not know yet, but it must mean something," I shouted.

Looking from the opposite edge of the stage gave me a better view of the suspended items, which seemed to be more animals on boards. They had strange designs underneath them.

Somehow, using this information, I needed to find a three-digit code to permit me to pull the trapdoor lever.

Once I had this, I knew I could save Sherlock Holmes and proceed.

HINTS
Difficult, turn to page 185
Medium, turn to page 190
Easy, turn to page 196
For solutions, turn to page 221

I pulled the lock off the hollow metal bar, wrenched it out of the way, and tugged the lever down as hard as I could, all in one smooth motion. My world seemed to collapse.

The lever had been marked "Trapdoors," yet perhaps I had not considered exactly what that plural had meant. Holmes's trapdoor had released, saving his life, yet one I had not noticed opened at the same time underneath me.

I fell.

After what seemed like forever, I plunged into a water-filled glass case—or should I say coffin—of my own. A grate slammed shut above me, trapping me underwater, and I immediately started looking around for a method of escape. Looking up, the grate consisted of thin slats of metal with just enough gap for me to squeeze most of my hand out of, but it easily prevented me from raising my mouth above the water.

The grate was secured in a way I could not even see. I was fast running out of breath, and only just noticed Holmes, who had landed himself on a well-placed pile of sandbags directly in front of me. He was safe, if wet, but looked truly afraid at our situation.

He leaped up, frantically examining our surroundings as I tried to calm down—the calmer I was, the longer before I needed another breath!

Holmes returned to me and shouted at the glass. "I have nothing to help you with. I can't get you out of there, Watson." He appeared truly distraught at our reversal of fortunes.

Was this my end? How could I get out of my glass prison?

In a flash of understanding—far more welcome than the flashes beginning to appear before my eyes—I realized that my priorities were wrong. I was only running out of time, because I needed to breathe. Given longer, Holmes might find a way to release me or get help to free me.

For now, all I needed was a way to breathe. But what was it?

"AFTER WHAT SEEMED LIKE FOREVER, I PLUNGED INTO A WATER-FILLED GLASS CASE—OR SHOULD I SAY COFFIN— OF MY OWN."

I still had the metal pipe that I had removed from the trapdoor lever.

I put it to my mouth, threaded it through the grate, blew out the excess water, and took a deliciously deep breath. I was going to survive, for now at least. Holmes visibly relaxed; he had seen no solution to this problem himself.

He approached the glass as I looked down, past the bar that I was still holding up, and leaned up against it. My relief was somewhat undermined by Holmes's nonchalance. Admittedly, my situation had improved, but I was still locked inside.

Eventually, Holmes realized this and stepped back, only to see the case budge slightly. I could see an idea come to him. He ran at the case, hoping to knock it over. It shuffled farther, but not enough. He raised his hand to me, one finger extended, and mouthed "one moment," before pacing out of my sight.

It seemed like forever that I was left waiting, once again. I was not short of breath, but I was far from comfortable stranded in ignorance of what was happening around me. Long minutes later, Holmes returned with a gaggle of police officers led by none other than Inspector Lestrade.

They approached and, with a great heave, pushed the case over. The glass shattered and exploded. I was free, if somewhat shaken from the experience. Regaining my composure, I stood up—with the help of my friend—and asked, "Inspector, how did you get here so fast?"

"We had a tip-off that Mr. Holmes here had lost his mind and was trying to murder you, Dr. Watson."

"Murder? Of course," Holmes realized. "Moriarty's plan had never been to kill me. It had been to engineer a situation whereby it looked like I had killed you, Watson. This whole thing was about setting me up."

"But why?"

"Killing me isn't part of the game. Killing me would have been too easy. To truly defeat me, he had to leave me alive, so that I would acknowledge defeat."

At last, we had overcome the final challenge set to us, but it was difficult to consider it a victory. Moriarty had escaped and was indeed still alive. Holmes had come close to recovering his own faculties, however, and perhaps the pressure of propping up our partnership would be off me for the moment.

It was a relief, enhanced by my knowledge of my own achievements, even if Holmes's unique method of congratulations would not exactly allow him to acknowledge them completely.

"Good job, Watson," he announced to the room, as much as to me. "Your skills are quite admirable. Certainly, very nearly to my own level."

"Surely you do not mean that, Holmes?" I smiled, honored by his statement, despite myself. Perhaps I had, in fact, learned enough to challenge the man himself!

"Of course not, but it seemed like something you'd like to hear."

Difficult Hints

The Game Is Afoot

Numbered telegrams.

221B Baker Street

The Cheriton Case
The M sealed it.

Carpe Diem
How is your Latin?

Chemical Experiment
Where else have I seen those chemicals?

Sheet Music
Notation translation.

Vinyl Etchings
Dash Dot Dash Dot.

Store Photographs
These cannot just be random locations.

Case Files
Perhaps there is an order to Holmes's chaotic filing system after all.

The Train to Cookham

Luggage Part I
Initially, I was stumped.

The Locked Case
There must be one case on board obviously different from the others.

Luggage Part II
All of the information I need is scattered around the coach.

Marked Map
Where else have I seen station names in the coach?

Train on a Train
Coaches and staff.

Meal Ingredients
How many servings are left?

Homestead Mansion

Portrait Puzzle
I do not think that I have seen this man's *face* before.

The Card Game
I do not recognize that card game layout.

CHINA LINEN PATTERN
The bedspread's unusual design matched the china plates in certain ways—but imperfectly.

KITCHEN JIGSAW
The oddball.

HOUSEHOLD CHORES
On the *face* of it, the detail of these chores is meaningless to me, although important for the staff, I'm sure.

AN UNUSUAL CLOCK
On the *face* of it, the clock appears broken—and yet it appears so well-maintained. Why would the master of the house not have had it fixed immediately?

THE HOMESTEAD FLOOR PLAN
If the floor plan is a map, is that a grid?

THE MIND PALACE

THE PAINTED SKY
Holmes's clue.

FLOATING LETTERS
Color translation.

FALLING HATS
Twins.

UNBURIED BODIES
The bodies are made up of particular repeated patterns, sizes, and colors. This has to be meaningful.

PARTICULAR MICE PUZZLE
Filling out the grid with the mice of various different colors, patterns, and sizes would be a great starting point.

THE OPERATING ROOM

WHICH WIG?
Count.

THE BLOATED BODY
Think of it like a doctor's favorite jigsaw.

BLOCKED TILES PUZZLE
The axes are important.

MEDICAL RECORDS PUZZLE
There was no Bolton, but perhaps another characteristic would be relevant here?

THE MATHEMATICAL ANESTHETIST
If I knew the weight of the patient in question, I could at least make a start.

THE KEY TO IT ALL
It was not originally in the room.

The Church

Sainted Windows and Statues
Are the statues the same saints as those named in the windows?

Organ's Octaves
Holmes's suggestion.

Stained Windows
Colorful?

A Very Odd Bible
Title.

Pew Puzzle
It is a grid! What are the coordinates?

The Fibbing Priest
The muddy shoes are the key.

The Cryptic Crypt
A does not equal 1 this time.

Scotland Yard

Notable Person Cards
Six suspects. But where to begin?

Confiscated Items
Are there any items of interest shown?

Patrolling London
Map it out.

Who Was Wanted?
X marks the spot.

Details of the Crime
Description.

The Vandal of Connaught Road
Last two.

Cell Number Five
A notable person.

The Cells

Roll the Die
Start at the start.

Eros
Take a spin at the cogs.

Harvey
Where to look next?

The Painted Bars
The letters behind the bars—are they numerals?

Happy Birthday
I recognize that decoration.

The Graffitied Wall
I need some direction.

THE CIRCUS

XELLDA'S ENIGMAS
There appear to be four answers.

THE PROPHETIC CYPHSTRESS
She is something of a riddle.

THE BEWILDER BOX
The panels—they contain the symbols as well!

THE STAR ATTRACTIONS
That design on the posters—does that not mean I should consult my ruler again?

BALL TOSS
This is more of a mental game than I originally gave it credit for.

A TICKET TO THE FINALE
Even in a circus, order is everything.

THE THEATER

COSTUME CONUNDRUM
Set list descriptions are the best place to start.

MATCHING CURTAINS
Perhaps I should start by pulling the curtains together to see the whole picture.

A BUMPY TIME
This is the blind leading the blind.

HANGING PROPS
Stack.

THE FINAL ESCAPE
A breathing apparatus.

BONUS PUZZLE
Can you identify the young boy in the carriage?

Medium Hints

The Game Is Afoot

Holmes has mentioned that the Armitage tale is for "another day." Interesting.

221B Baker Street

The Cheriton Case
The similarity was glaring.

Carpe Diem
Carpe diem means "seize the day."

Chemical Experiment
The colors of the chemicals are hidden around the room.

Sheet Music
Musical notes can be read as letters, but reading this particular music as words appears nonsensical.

Vinyl Etchings
The series of dots and dashes are clearly reminiscent of something else I have found in the room.

Store Photographs
I had recently been to the store run by Mr. and Mrs. Bond and found it to be a most pleasant experience. The others, however, were not recognizable to me as being located nearby. There must be a reason Holmes had traveled to each of them and taken these photographs, because he is not the sentimental type.

Case Files
Drawing upon Holmes's previous exploits was a clever trick indeed.

The Train to Cookham

Luggage Part I
Perhaps the names are a clue in themselves?

The Locked Case
If none of the cases in the other compartment open, perhaps the answer lies elsewhere?

Luggage Part II
Thinking logically should solve this one.

Marked Map
Of course, the station map with the missing place names. These stations must fill those gaps.

Train on a Train
I have the information for a train traveling from Cookham to

Loudwater. Perhaps those same rules could apply to the train from Maidenhead to Cookham?

MEAL INGREDIENTS
Now that I know the staff numbers on a train from Maidenhead to Cookham, I should be able to work out the amounts of each meal eaten on the journey.

HOMESTEAD MANSION

PORTRAIT PUZZLE
Not his face, but his name is familiar.

THE CARD GAME
It's nonsensical! No game could possibly lead to such a layout. There must be another reason the deck has been arranged in such a manner.

CHINA LINEN PATTERN
There are thirty plates and thirty individual squares on the bedspread. There must be something in the layout.

KITCHEN JIGSAW
Returning the pots to their proper configuration might reveal something.

HOUSEHOLD CHORES
"The master of the house is interested in only the total amount of hours worked per day for all staff combined." Why? Time is of the essence!

AN UNUSUAL CLOCK
Two o'clock on Wednesday. The number and day must be of significance to be so clearly marked.

THE HOMESTEAD FLOOR PLAN
That grid must be useful, but where to *start*?

THE MIND PALACE

THE PAINTED SKY
Objectively, the items Holmes conjured should not be those colors.

FLOATING LETTERS
The colors behind the letters seem familiar.

FALLING HATS
Am I seeing double?

UNBURIED BODIES
The names are all six letters long, and each body has three identifiable attributes: their size, their color, and their pattern. There are five of each.

PARTICULAR MICE PUZZLE
The hats around the outside; there must be something important about the two that I earlier identified as being different from the others. Are their locations signaling something?

The Operating Room

Which Wig?
Matching the wigs I can see to the catalog seems appropriate.

The Bloated Body
Once the picture is complete, what is missing?

Blocked Tiles Puzzle
I appear to have two coordinates.

Medical Records Puzzle
There must be something else in the room to help me *identify* what I should be searching for.

The Mathematical Anesthetist
Of course, I have already identified a patient in this room whose weight I know.

The Key to It All
Holmes had always been a master of sleight of hand.

The Church

Sainted Windows and Statues
There must be a way to identify the statues using the information I already know about the saints.

Organ's Octaves
I already know the colored keys are the important ones. So, what to do with them?

Stained Windows
The windows are not the multicolored stained glass often found in churches.

A Very Odd Bible
The subjects of the tales seem familiar.

Pew Puzzle
Ah, the key references map onto the pew grid perfectly. But they do not mean anything. Is there anything else I have discovered that I have not yet made use of?

The Fibbing Priest
When was the funeral scheduled for?

The Cryptic Crypt
There are twenty-six graves, and two other lots of twenty-six to be discovered, too.

Scotland Yard

Notable Person Cards
Can I eliminate any of the suspects? The information must be elsewhere in the file.

Patrolling London
Tracking the officers' patrol routes

might be tedious, but good police work often is.

CONFISCATED ITEMS
How many items have been illustrated?

WHO WAS WANTED?
Following the instructions should lead to the Knife's place of work, allowing for me to identify his real name.

DETAILS OF THE CRIME
Five crimes were committed.

THE VANDAL OF CONNAUGHT ROAD
This could apply to many of the notable persons, but only one of the remaining suspects.

CELL NUMBER FIVE
Did Holmes know who had been in the cell previously?

THE CELLS

ROLL THE DIE
Roll up, roll up.

EROS
The grid indicates that the cogs are important. Do I have anything to input into the "IN"?

HARVEY
I found the name Harvey on another

object in the room. What could that be telling me?

THE PAINTED BARS
The paint is curious. At times it is on only the left half, at other times on the right half, and occasionally it runs the whole way across. That must be meaningful.

HAPPY BIRTHDAY
After all that trouble they did not even bother to purchase new candles. Unless . . .

THE GRAFFITIED WALL
Both of the sequences I discovered are thirteen entries long. They have to be related to each other in some way.

THE CIRCUS

XELLDA'S ENIGMAS
The riddles—if that is what they are—must be related to something else in this bizarre circus.

THE PROPHETIC CYPHSTRESS
The riddles' answers led me to the tarot cards. But what should I do with that information?

THE BEWILDER BOX
The object of the circus game is to fit the pieces into a cube. I could not see a reason why I should not do the same.

THE STAR ATTRACTIONS
I cannot quite *figure* out what I should be looking at, personally.

BALL TOSS
The circus is especially tidy, except for these balls littered around the place. Did someone leave them out intentionally?

A TICKET TO THE FINALE
Four numbers are all I need.

THE THEATER

COSTUME CONUNDRUM
The descriptions of the acts are not much help. A water escape? What does that mean? There must be more help for me elsewhere.

MATCHING CURTAINS
The knots are all associated with a letter.

A BUMPY TIME
The SH should tell me where I need to look for answers.

HANGING PROPS
I now have three letters, but what to do with the patterns below the animals?

THE FINAL ESCAPE
Do I have anything on me that could be of use?

BONUS PUZZLE
He appeared to have an extraordinarily precocious interest in art for one so young.

Easy Hints

The Game Is Afoot

The lines on the steps seem reminiscent of something, especially when looked at in combination.

221B Baker Street

The Cheriton Case
Something links the itinerary with the handwritten card that was staring me in the face.

Carpe Diem
Where else had I seen a particular day in the room?

Chemical Experiment
The letters I am left with are scrambled, but with some fiddling I think I can spell something notable.

Sheet Music
Those numbers that Holmes has scribbled over the music must mean something. Perhaps they are some kind of cipher?

Vinyl Etchings
Of course! Morse code. I will have to use Holmes's table to help me translate.

Store Photographs
Ah, the names. But they are scattered somewhat haphazardly. How should I ascertain the correct order?

Case Files
The answers have all led to the case files. Perhaps tracing the files I have uncovered will shed some light on the situation.

The Train to Cookham

Luggage Part I
That white suitcase has certainly traveled a long way.

The Locked Case
The answer was staring me in the face the whole time!

Luggage Part II
Perhaps if I draw a logic grid in my case notebook and start to analyze the information that Holmes has supplied me with, I will be able to match the various suitcases with their owners and journeys.

Marked Map
The map is to scale, so I should be able to use the journey distances to correctly fill in the gaps. The journey between High Wycombe and

Maidenhead is the longest, so they might be the best place to start.

TRAIN ON A TRAIN

Ah, I know the distance and number of stops needed to travel from Maidenhead to Cookham, now that I have fixed the station map. If I use that information, along with the instructions given, surely I could determine the makeup of a train traveling between the two places.

MEAL INGREDIENTS

There are eight ingredients that it appears I should pay particular attention to. However, that would only leave me with eight numbers divided into two series of three and five numbers, respectively. Could the numbers be substituted with anything to make more sense?

HOMESTEAD MANSION

PORTRAIT PUZZLE

The mother is the key! A clever play on words indeed.

THE CARD GAME

It appears the entire deck is on show. Unless I've *missed* something?

CHINA LINEN PATTERN

Perhaps it is not about how the patterns created in the china and the bedspread are different, but how they are the same?

KITCHEN JIGSAW

There are certainly too many pots, pans, and utensils here to fit into the cabinet. And what could those strange markings signify?

HOUSEHOLD CHORES

Ah, the clock upstairs was set to the wrong time, and the wrong day? What if I combined the information given here with that?

AN UNUSUAL CLOCK

There has been only one other place in the house where I have seen a day combined with a number of hours. What—or when—would adding the information together get me?

THE HOMESTEAD FLOOR PLAN

N. E. W. S. Abbreviations?

THE MIND PALACE

THE PAINTED SKY

Why mention the objects from an old case at all? Unless they were some kind of cipher. There must be a method to this madness!

FLOATING LETTERS

I have a series of colors, and the letters associated with them. When combined with the information I had just learned from the painted objects, what am I left with? Words I have seen recently, I am sure.

FALLING HATS
Not all of the hats are paired with another.

UNBURIED BODIES
Many of the same letters are repeated throughout the last names. Perhaps the attributes are connected to the six letters that make up each name?

PARTICULAR MICE PUZZLE
The hats have led me to one particular mouse, and it has three attributes that can lead me to six letters. But they are nonsensical. Can they be rearranged to a meaningful name?

THE OPERATING ROOM

WHICH WIG?
There are not as many wigs as there are catalog entries.

THE BLOATED BODY
The pictured body appears to be a textbook case of a number of different maladies.

BLOCKED TILES PUZZLE
The tiles appear to act as some kind of drain. Now that I have a grid position,

what would happen if some kind of liquid landed there?

MEDICAL RECORDS PUZZLE
Something else in the room appears on one of the cards.

THE MATHEMATICAL ANESTHETIST
Once the mathematics had been completed, I was left with a string of numbers. How could I translate them into something more relevant?

THE KEY TO IT ALL
I had never once known Holmes to be worried about his odor before.

THE CHURCH

SAINTED WINDOWS AND STATUES
Aha! I finally be*held* the connection between them. But what to do with that information? I am not completely directionless.

ORGAN'S OCTAVES
I have seen a combination of numbers and letters somewhere else in the church, where one normally would not expect to see them while seated here.

STAINED WINDOWS
The characters in each window almost tell a tale.

A Very Odd Bible
Of course, the windows!

Pew Puzzle
Ah yes, the statues. And the stories are nonsensical, but the saints appear in them. Multiple times, at that. Such repetition is not necessary for good storytelling. Unless there is a meaning behind it? Which direction to go in next, I wondered.

The Fibbing Priest
Why is the calendar empty?

The Cryptic Crypt
The ages and initials shown on the graves are of the utmost importance.

Scotland Yard

Notable Person Cards
I have to work through all of the information I have and perhaps I will be left with just one suspect.

Confiscated Items
There is one fewer item illustrated than listed. That must be the item that was returned.

Patrolling London
I know who discovered the unfortunate McAvoy. Can I determine when and where they did it?

Who Was Wanted?
It was good to know this dangerous fellow was now off the streets.

Details of the Crime
Whose criminal record matches?

The Vandal of Connaught Road
Are there any clues about the suspect's place of work?

Cell Number Five
Of course, the cards indicate that Greaves was being held there. But how would that have helped Holmes?

The Cells

Roll the Die
STARTing at the bottom left should help. And the – seem to indicate the ends of words. But halfway through, the sequence of recognizable words ends and a series of random letters begins.

Eros
I have a string of letters. It appears like I should translate them through the cog alphabet. If I turn the input cog clockwise, which way will the output cog turn?

Harvey
Thankfully, it appears the shard of mirror is not to be used for any

nefarious purposes. It is merely a symbol of what to do next.

THE PAINTED BARS
Ah, those are numerals! And they match the information I already have. It appears Holmes was right and I must split them. Will the paint help me do that?

HAPPY BIRTHDAY
Yes, the ruler matches the symbols on the wall. They must be of interest here.

THE GRAFFITIED WALL
Parkinson had tapped the red X. Perhaps that is where I need to start. I now have directions and lengths to move in.

THE CIRCUS

XELLDA'S ENIGMAS
The token set us on the path to Xellda. Tracing the token back to its roots might help me answer these riddles—and decide where to turn next.

THE PROPHETIC CYPHSTRESS
Are the cards symbolic in some way?

THE BEWILDER BOX
There is no obvious way that they should fit together. They do, however,

all have odd etchings in each of the corners. If I start matching the lines together, perhaps recognizable shapes will appear?

THE STAR ATTRACTIONS
Ha. It is the cipher that Holmes cracked during the unfortunate case involving the Cubitts. Whoever has designed this clearly knows our *colorful* history together well.

BALL TOSS
The colors! That is what was frustrating me. The posters are the exact same colors as the balls and their tubes.

A TICKET TO THE FINALE
The tickets are all numbered, too.

THE THEATER

COSTUME CONUNDRUM
Ah yes, the posters we saw in the lobby!

MATCHING CURTAINS
Matching the knots to the animals will mean that they are each associated with a letter as well.

A BUMPY TIME
Of course, the ruler has a braille alphabet on it.

HANGING PROPS

Perhaps if I do something with the patterns on the correct boards—add or subtract them from each other—I might be able to create something recognizable? It has nothing to do with braille, anyway.

THE FINAL ESCAPE

The slats in the grate are too narrow for my head, but I think I could fit something else through there.

BONUS PUZZLE

He was unlikely to have traveled far from his hometown.

THE GAME IS AFOOT

First, I discovered the order of the telegrams. There were only two options for a starting point—telegrams 1 and 2—and two for an ending point—4 and 14. Reading them closely, I realized that Holmes's hint about the Armitage case—that it was a "story for another day"—meant that I could discount those telegrams. I was left with the telegrams numbered 1, 5, and 14.

Following his instructions, I inserted the digits into the final sentence: "Of 17 from your entry, stack step 1, step 5, and step 14 from bottom to top to grant access."

I rushed back downstairs and sketched the designs on the face of the steps, one on top of the other. Seeing the three digits 415, I knew I had the code to grant me access to the study.

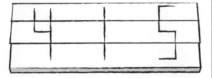

221B BAKER STREET

THE CHERITON CASE

The handwriting on the card was a direct match with that on the itinerary. Mrs. Cheriton was clearly the author of both, and the Cheritons themselves were the culprits.

CARPE DIEM

"Seize the day" led me back to the odd calendar that I had seen earlier, with the *day* circled. Upon seizing it, I knew I was on the right track.

CHEMICAL EXPERIMENT

The initial step was to return to the "first clue" I noticed in the room: the chemical experiment that I had seen upon entry. I matched the chemicals with their colors from the notes scattered throughout the room and then added or subtracted places in the alphabet from the letters given, as per Holmes's instructions. This gave me:

Black = Iodine = $I - 8 = A$
Red = Phosphorus = $P + 2 = R$
Yellow = Iron oxide = $X + 5 + 10 = M$
Green = Copper chloride =
   $C - 8 - 6 = O$
Blue = Copper sulfate = $S + 2 + 5 = Z$
Silver = Mercury = $M - 8 + 15 = T$

These letters are an anagram for MOZART.

SHEET MUSIC

I had noticed the word "Mozart"

elsewhere in the room, so I turned my attention to the three annotated scraps of sheet music that Holmes had left for me. I swiftly understood that the numbers worked as a cipher in the exact same manner as the chemical experiment had. Thus, the first note of the Mozart piece—an E—should be transcribed eleven places along the alphabet, from the fifth to the sixteenth letter: P. Helpfully, Sherlock had left another scrap of paper that told me that a # symbol increased the transcription by a further five places.

After a few moments I had it, and I realized with mounting excitement that the words I had revealed were the names of some of Holmes's cases. The pieces were beginning to fall into place. The words were:

"Painter, Harris, Fletcher, Ormstein, Painter, and Hatherley."

Incidentally, the other two pieces, when translated, did not impress me. They read:

"Did you not think you should check the chemical experiment Watson" and "You are taking too long on this puzzle Watson hurry up now."

Vinyl Etchings

Holmes's letter clearly indicated that after music I should turn my attention to the vinyl record. Once I realized that the etchings he had made in the record were Morse code, the job of translation was a relatively simple one.

The fact that more case names were revealed only confirmed to me that I was still on the right track. The cases were: CHERITON / BASKERVILLE / REGAN / HANSFORD / REGAN / PELTZER / MORTON.

Store Photographs

Examining the photographs more closely, I noticed the names of the proprietors matched our case files exactly. Quickly, I also realized five of the pictures seemed to have been manipulated with a number placed on them: the order the names should appear. These were as follows:

1—Bond
2—O'Riley
3—Mitchell
4—Lewis
5—Hamer

Case Files

The final piece of the puzzle: everything else in the room led me back to our old cases. I stared at them, nonplussed at first, I confess. But as I considered what Holmes was trying to tell me, I recognized an order in the file names I had been left with. If I physically followed the pattern of the answers, crude numbers appeared, in much the same way as they had on the staircase.

The sheet music has the number 9, the vinyl Morse code gave me a 3, and the postcards a 2: so 9-3-2. The significance of these three numbers, however, escaped me. It was only upon returning to the letter Holmes had written to me that I noticed his final exhortation: "but not necessarily dated in this order." An odd turn of phrase, to be sure. It only made sense if he was pointing me toward the word *dated*.

Shaking my head at my ignorance, I returned to the case files. Sure enough, there was one whose date contained all three numbers. Lewis. 3/92. I grasped the file eagerly.

THE TRAIN TO COOKHAM

LUGGAGE PART I
The first—and most obvious—clue was that Owen's case was marked as traveling from Paris to Berlin. The British rail system is certainly first class, but I knew a domestic commuter train

could never have made it to either destination. As I pondered this, I also noticed that the first letters of each name, when arranged in a certain way, spelled out WATSON. That was just the level of attention to detail Holmes expected of me, and it was too much of a coincidence to have occurred by chance.

THE LOCKED CASE
Of course, my own suitcase! Holmes has taught me time and again not to leap to assumptions without considering every eventuality.

LUGGAGE PART II
The most obvious place to start was with the luggage conundrum that Holmes had created in his letter. Once I had diligently worked through the information that Holmes had helpfully supplied me with, it became clear that the only possible combination was this:

Name	Route	Distance	Color of Suitcase	Suitcase Size (1-6)
Abbey	High Wycombe-Loudwater	½ mile	Blue	4
Nicholson	Marlow-Bourne End	2 miles	Red	2
Owen	Paris-Berlin	545 miles	White	3
Smith	High Wycombe-Maidenhead	7 miles	Green	1
Trevor	Cookham-Loudwater	4 miles	Black	5
Willis	High Wycombe-Marlow	6 miles	Brown	6

MARKED MAP

Using the strange ruler that Holmes had left for me, I was swiftly able to replace the missing station names in their correct places on the map. I was left with this:

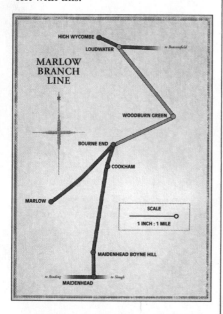

MARLOW BRANCH LINE

HIGH WYCOMBE
LOUDWATER
to Beaconsfield
WOODBURN GREEN
BOURNE END
COOKHAM
MARLOW
MAIDENHEAD BOYNE HILL
to Reading
to Slough
MAIDENHEAD

SCALE
1 INCH : 1 MILE

At this moment, I was not sure why this knowledge would be important, but I had to trust that this puzzle Holmes had left me had a logic to it, and so I moved on.

TRAIN ON A TRAIN

I returned to my coach to ponder my next steps. Flicking through my notebook, my eyes lit upon the words "Maidenhead to Cookham = ?" Of course! I now knew that Maidenhead to Cookham was a 2½-mile journey and involved only two stops, the first at Maidenhead Boyne Hill and the second at Cookham itself.

According to the strange rules supplied along with the train set, a train traveling on that journey would be made up of:

   5 passenger coaches
   1 dining coach
   1 luggage coach
   2 goods coaches

Its staff would therefore consist of:

   5 ticket inspectors
   1 waiter
   1 train guard
   4 haulers
   1 chef
   2 drivers

Now, what should be done with this information?

MEAL INGREDIENTS

The only other place in the coach where I could recall seeing members of staff mentioned was in the decidedly odd series of notices regarding meals. Returning to them, I analyzed them each anew. Armed with my recently discovered information, I could ascertain that on a train from Maidenhead to Cookham, the following meals would be consumed:

   5 ticket inspectors = 5 hamburgers and 5 fudge desserts

1 waiter = 1 pork ribs
1 train guard = 1 chicken pie
4 haulers = 4 beef pies and
4 mother's cookies
1 chef = 1 hamburger and 1 mother's cookies
2 drivers = 2 goulash and 2 mother's cookies

Cross-referencing with the overly detailed menu, I could tell that the ingredient servings used would be as follows:

7 baking powder, 12 beef, 14 butter, 1 chicken, 12 chocolate, 5 corn, 9 flour, 2 garlic, 7 green bell pepper, 5 milk, 7 oats, 14 onion, 7 paprika, 1 pork, 26 salt, 14 sugar, 6 tomato, 7 vinegar, 14 water

In his message from management, Samuel Hardington asked specifically about eight ingredients, and I was drawn to the particular manner in which they were laid out:

Onion, Tomato, Milk
Beef, Green Bell Pepper, Salt, Butter, Chocolate

The amounts left of each were:
20, 8, 5
13, 15, 21, 14, 20

I must confess it took me several minutes to discover the final piece

of the puzzle. The numbers were a cipher! Using a simple alphanumeric substitution in which the numbers represented the letters of the alphabet—where a = 1 and z = 26— I came up with two words:
THE MOUNT

HOMESTEAD MANSION

PORTRAIT PUZZLE
I dashed back downstairs briefly to refresh my memory, but I was indeed correct. Thomas Harris's grandson was John, and John's mother was Emily Watt. It was surely too much of a coincidence for John Watt's son to be highlighted in such a way. I was the welcome party, and thus I could feel somewhat more relaxed about my furtive investigations.

THE CARD GAME
Counting the number of cards displayed, I realized that there were only fifty-one on the table. After laboriously taking stock of the cards in front of me, I determined that the seven of hearts was missing. And I had seen the word MISSING elsewhere in the room. Of course, the artwork! And hearts is next to E.

CHINA LINEN PATTERN
It was clear that the types of pattern on the china plates had been painstakingly

sewn into this unusual bedspread. The Willow Blue was unmistakable, but the Christmas holly, the Byzance, the Arris, and the botanical decoration were all there as well. I confess, I had to bring the linen downstairs with me to hang next to the china plates before the answer came to me.

In sixteen of the thirty instances, the patterns were the same on both the china plates and the bedspread. The second row, first column, for example, contained a distinctive Byzance design on both occasions. I removed all of the unmatched plates from the dresser, and I was clearly left with a letter and a number: S3. I could only hope that its meaning would become clearer to me as I discovered more of this unusual house's secrets.

KITCHEN JIGSAW

I set about replacing the various kitchen detritus in the cabinet where I believed it belonged (my efforts are below, but I'm sure there were other ways I could have done it), and sure enough, there was one pan left over. After all of my effort, I realized I could have completed the challenge far quicker—the pan in question was the only object that took up an odd number of squares, and so must have been the oddball.

Muttering to myself for not seeing that sooner, I took the ruler out from where I had placed it in my pocket earlier and measured the line drawn on the pan against the markings on it. Sure enough, the line was the same length as the one on the ruler marked S1.

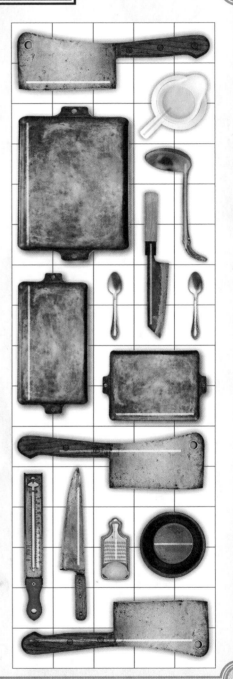

Household Chores

The "master of the house" was only interested in the "total number of hours worked per day for all staff combined." If he was, I assumed I should be as well.

Gardening was the easiest place to start. It must happen once a week, when John was in—a Friday—for four hours. He must also clean the house that day, because they must each do so once per week. And as the most experienced chef that day (only Mary is in at the same time), he must cook as well. Because he must have also worked the longest that day, he is also expected to do the dish washing, too: a total of nine hours of work for the poor fellow. Mary also attends the house on a Friday but is bizarrely left with no tasks to perform. Presumably, she can just watch John toil with her feet up.

The only other weekday on which Mary is present is a Monday, so she must clean the house on that day. Leonard also works on a Monday, and is a better chef than Mary, so he must attend to both the cooking and the dish washing on that day.

Mary—who appears to be getting away with performing remarkably little actual work—is also needed on a Sunday, which is one of the laundry days. Shirley is also available for chores on the sabbath. Mary, therefore, is chef for the day, while Shirley washes the clothes and Mary must finish the day by dish washing.

Thursday is an unusual day in that Anna must toil in solitude for the whole day. She must take charge of the cooking, dish washing, and cleaning for that day.

Saturday sees Leonard and Anna report for duty, and as only cooking and dish washing take place that day, Leonard may as well head straight home again, leaving Anna in charge of the kitchen.

Anna also works on a Tuesday alongside Shirley, and because she is already cleaning the house on a Thursday, Shirley must take charge of both the cleaning and the dish washing that day, while Anna cooks.

The final day still to be determined is Wednesday, which sees Leonard and Shirley working. Because Leonard is the chef, Shirley must wash the clothes. However, by elimination Wednesday must be Leonard's turn to clean the house, which also means that he must do the dish washing.

The hours worked each day are thus:

Monday: 4.5 hours
Tuesday: 6 hours
Wednesday: 8 hours
Thursday: 5 hours
Friday: 9 hours
Saturday: 2.5 hours
Sunday: 4 hours

An Unusual Clock

Intuitively, I knew that the time and day shown on the clock face must combine with the other place in the house where I had seen a length of time and a day—the household chores. On Wednesday, eight hours of work take place in the house. If the hour hand is thus rotated by eight, it lands upon ten o'clock, which gives me another letter and number (in this case a Roman numeral): W10.

The Homestead Floor Plan

After solving all of the mysterious house's puzzles, I was left with four clues: E7, S3, S1, and W10. It did not take long for me to deduce that these must be directions: East 7, South 3, South 1, and West 10. They must relate to the map. Returning to it, I noticed the word that I had thought marked my entry point: "Start." It was not telling me where I was when I found the map, it was telling me where to start my movements!

Following the instructions led me to the square marked "Homes."

The Mind Palace

The Painted Sky

I began with Holmes's own clue—he said "Cat. Spade. Knife. Pipe. Heart. Umbrella." These were highly specific objects and clearly in a certain order. What's more, I had seen those objects before when they had appeared painted in the sky. The colors seemed important, because each object had its own hue. Taken in order the objects translated to:

Red. Turquoise. Black. Pink. Silver. Blue.

Floating Letters

Thinking back, I realized that during my strange trip I had seen flashes of letters in colors that matched the colors of the objects exactly. These were:

Gold = P
Turquoise= T
Silver = R
Blue = Y
Orange = O
Cream = E
Red = S
Pink = A
Yellow = C
Purple = H
Black = M

Matching these letters against the sequence of colors I had just identified, I discovered the following:

STMARY

St. Mary . . . my mind leaped to the map of London that I had seen. One of the landmarks was St. Mary's Hospital. That must be the location that we needed!

FALLING HATS

As the hat fell and morphed into multiple replicas, I realized a pattern was appearing. Not all of the hats were identical, but instead each hat had a pair that was identical to it. Only two hats broke the sequence.

UNBURIED BODIES

Now that I had my location, I could turn my attention to the person that I needed to identify. I had a strong suspicion that the strangely patterned bodies might be the key here.

I wrote down everything I knew about them, and was left with the following list of attributes:

Very small, Checked pattern, Cream, E. FERBON

Very small, Spotted pattern, Cream, I. BELFER

Small, Zigzag pattern, Brown, C. STREEK

Small, Checked pattern, Green, S. BONNER

Medium, Wavy pattern, Cream, F. FASCER

Medium, Zigzag pattern, Gray, T. BLACKE

Medium, Plain, Green, R. BEACON

Large, Checked pattern, Blue, D. DOTAIN

Large, Plain, Blue, O. TOADIE

Giant, Wavy pattern, Cream, O. FOSTER

Giant, Spotted pattern, Blue, B. TOILED

Unattached, M. FRANKO

Unattached, B. BOLTON

Unattached, T. BALOCK

Unattached, P. LAPPEL

Unattached, F. ROOFER

Unattached, S. DOTTEO

My instincts told me that there was something unusual about the last names. They all had only six letters for one thing, and there seemed to be many of the same letters repeated over and over again. Using some mental acuity worthy of Sherlock Holmes himself, I understood that each attribute represented two letters. All three attributes combined to create each last name. Thus:

Checked = NO

Plain = EO

Spotted = EL

Wavy = FS

Zigzag = EK

Blue = DI

Brown = ST

Cream = ER

Green = BN

Gray = BL

Very small = BF
Small = ER
Medium = AC
Large = AT
Giant = OT

PARTICULAR MICE PUZZLE
Given the rules that I knew about the mice puzzle grid, I fairly swiftly filled the blank spaces with mice of all colors and sizes, as follows:

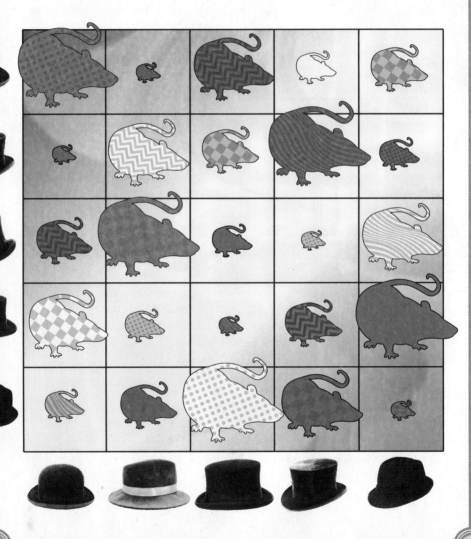

The hats I had noticed earlier were arrayed around the outside of the grid, and I suspected that the two lonely hats without a pair must be of paramount importance. They lay on Row 3, Column 2. The mouse in that position was Giant, Checked, and Gray.

Given what I knew about the attributes and their associations with letters, I "translated" the mouse to find the letters:

OTNOBL

Alas, those letters were nonsensical. However, it was only a short time until I made my final breakthrough—one of the names that was unattached to the bodies was a direct anagram for the letters I had!

BOLTON. So, B. Bolton was our man.

THE OPERATING ROOM

WHICH WIG?
I began with the wigs, because they seemed the objects most out of place in this odd little room. It became quickly apparent that there was one fewer wig than catalog entries—this had to be of significance. Swiftly, I matched the wigs displayed to the descriptions and they all matched, except for one:

X9—Long Straight Red

THE BLOATED BODY
Returning to the cut-up picture of the body, I reassembled the pieces and was left with a grotesque image. Fortunately, it was not nearly the worst I had seen in my career.

The body was affected by a number of afflictions, albeit not any that I immediately recognized, which concerned me as a man of science. It was then that I realized that the cards showing illnesses I had never heard of matched the symptoms on the body precisely, all except for one. The malady named kallengroit was not displayed. It was labeled Y1.

BLOCKED TILES PUZZLE

I now had two grid coordinates, X9 and Y1. These had to refer to the numbers and letters around the tiles I had seen previously. I examined the spot—it seemed just like the rest of the grid. I stood, nonplussed, trying to fathom the way forward. It was then that I remembered the pipes overhead. Something was designed to fall here, and the blockages would stop it from expanding around the entire grid. I had to use my imagination, but this is what would be created by the spreading liquid:

Ignoring the lines connecting number to number, I was clearly left with three digits—857.

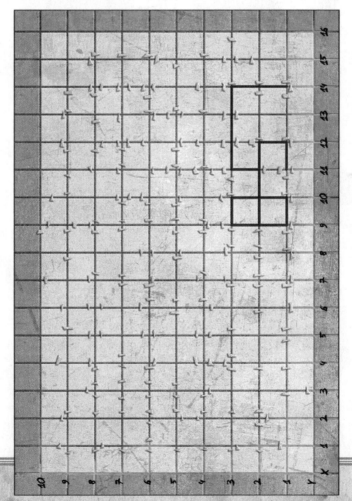

MEDICAL RECORDS PUZZLE

The number 857 was one of the ID numbers on the medical records! I rushed over to the cabinet and grabbed the card triumphantly. It belonged to Mr. R. Butcher.

THE MATHEMATICAL ANESTHETIST

The anesthetic poster was complex, but now that I knew Mr. R. Butcher's weight, I could surely discover the numbers referenced on it. After some calculation, I concluded that the correct amounts were 10 units of ether, 15 units of cocaine, 19 units of nitrous oxide, 248 units of ammonium nitrate, and 24 units of water.

The poster asked me to find numbers from this information and, following its instructions, I came up with 19 20 10 15 8 14 19.

The final piece of the puzzle was given to me by the poster's cryptic use of the term "A1 student." That indicated to me that I was supposed to translate the numbers using a simple alphanumeric substitution: A = 1, B = 2, and so on. This gave me the letters STJOHNS.

St. John's—the name of the church from the map of London I saw in Sherlock's mind palace!

THE KEY TO IT ALL

I had thought it odd at the time, but Holmes was a man of so many peculiarities that I passed it off as nothing more than just one more. However, he was not retrieving a mint from the receptionist's desk but instead the key that we would need to make our escape.

THE CHURCH

SAINTED WINDOWS AND STATUES

Each saint held an item in his hands, some kind of motif that they were associated with, I assumed. They were:
Apple—Saint Alban
Book—Saint Benno
Feather—Saint Felix
Sword—Saint Siricius

The statues were all holding the same items, so I knew which was which. I therefore had a direction associated with each saint:
Saint Alban is looking to his left.
Saint Benno is looking down.
Saint Felix is looking to his right.
Saint Siricius is looking up.

ORGAN'S OCTAVES

As Holmes had so helpfully pointed out, the colored keys of the organ must be important, although just at the moment I could not be sure exactly how. Noting the keys' letters and numbers down, I found:
Blue—C3

Green—B5
Red—C6
Yellow—G6

STAINED WINDOWS

I had been in a fair share of churches in my time, and stained-glass windows have always been a wonder to behold. However, the beauty of them was often to be found in their multicolor glory. These, although stunning in their own way, were all of one color. What was more, glancing down at my notes, I appreciated the fact that I had seen the colors elsewhere. The four colors were the same as the organ keys. I was certain that this was no coincidence but, once again, its final meaning still eluded me.

A VERY ODD BIBLE

I skimmed quickly through the rest of the Bible but could see nothing more out of place other than the extremely odd bookmarked pages— at least to the eyes of this layperson. The stories were so strange, however, that I could make neither heads nor tails of it. My eyes drifted upward in exasperation, and alighted once more on the monochromatic windows—the Samaritan of Jericho, the Shepherd, the Musician, the Wolf and the Eagle—the characters were all there!

Suddenly, I had new purpose. Each color was now associated with a story, a letter, and a number, as follows:

"The Samaritan of Jericho"—Blue—C3
"The Shepherd"—Red—C6
"The Musician"—Yellow—G6
"The Wolf and the Eagle"—Green—B5

PEW PUZZLE

The musical notations reminded me of something, and, after a brief pause, I came up with the answer—the pews! They were marked with the same numbers and letters, as if they were grid references. Turning back to my sketch, I marked the grid points in the hopes of being hit with a revelation. Alas, I was disappointed. I was missing something.

I sat on the nearest pew and looked around me, before my eyes alighted on the statues. Of course—I also had a direction associated with each saint. The tales were mostly nonsensical, but the saints all appeared in them. Perhaps for every time they appeared, I was to follow their direction?

For example, in "The Samaritan of Jericho," the saints appear in the following order: Alban, Alban, Siricius, Siricius, Felix, Felix, Benno, Benno, Benno, Benno. This would translate to: left, left, up, up, right, right, down, down, down, down.

I quickly began sketching again.

I had it: 913.

Image shown on page 214.

THE FIBBING PRIEST

There was nothing in the calendar for this morning, meaning there could have been no funeral. What is more, the area around the path, where one would assume a new burial would take place, was well maintained. It was only farther into the grounds that abundant mud was present.

THE CRYPTIC CRYPT

I hoped that the numbers on the crypt would translate directly into letters. Unfortunately, using the simple A = 1 formula that I had so recently come across, I obtained LBSVXZ. This was clearly not a word.

I was stumped for where else to turn until I remembered what Holmes had said about the graves. There were twenty-six, the same number of letters in the alphabet. Surely, this could not be a coincidence. Studying the graves further, I noticed something even more unusual. No unfortunate soul buried in this graveyard had lived beyond the age of twenty-six.

I scribbled the information on the graves into my notebook and realized two further pieces of information. There were twenty-six different initials and twenty-six different ages represented. Rearranging them into age order gave me the cipher below:

I decided to substitute the numbers on the crypt for the initials of the first names, which gave me MCAVOY. Indeed, J. McAvoy was buried right there, next to the crypt itself. He must be our man.

1	K. Ocknell	1821-1822	14	L. Palmer	1841-1855
2	C. Grove	1891-1893	15	N. Physick	1851-1866
3	D. Abbey	1842-1845	16	Z. Eserin	1878-1894
4	U. Savage	1850-1854	17	R. Simes	1833-1850
5	S. Lights	1849-1854	18	T. Green	1825-1843
6	Q. Jupest	1854-1860	19	O. Butler	1847-1866
7	F. Hampton	1887-1894	20	X. Rubens	1871-1891
8	B. Harrison	1834-1842	21	J. McAvoy	1873-1894
9	E. Frodsham	1831-1840	22	A. Oliver	1837-1859
10	H. Bennett	1882-1892	23	W. Harris	1856-1879
11	G. Rideout	1836-1847	24	V. Osman	1844-1868
12	M. Fawley	1839-1851	25	I. Sparks	1869-1894
13	P. Gordan	1828-1841	26	Y. Sanders	1859-1885

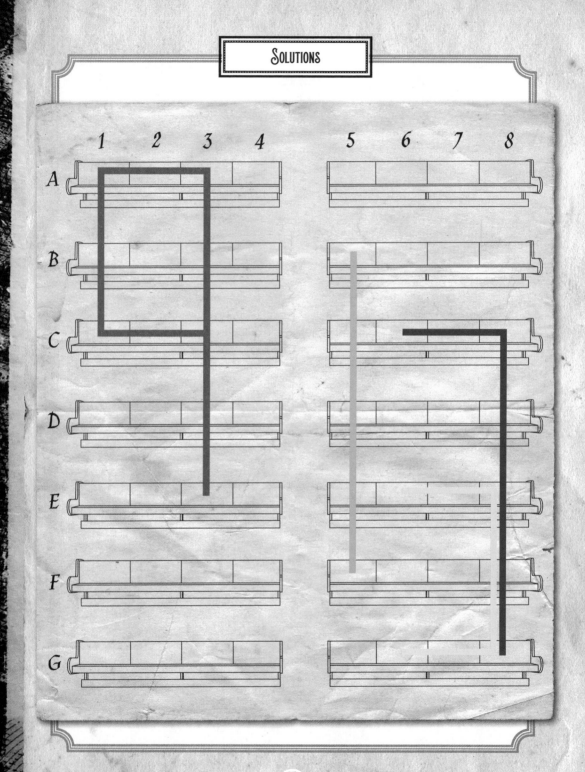

SCOTLAND YARD

NOTABLE PERSON CARDS
The cards I discovered in the cabinet showed the police had narrowed their search down to six potential suspects. Right now, I could not say who the prime suspect was, but I had the feeling that the information on the cards would help me prove five of them innocent.

CONFISCATED ITEMS
There are twelve items listed, but only eleven images. The item not shown must be the one that the police returned to the innocent party. A quick analysis proved that the tobacco was missing.

Checking the notable person cards, I noticed that Mark Johnson was a tobacconist. The police must have proved Johnson was not the murderer.

PATROLLING LONDON
With some quick calculation, I worked out the exact timings of the policemen's patrols, as follows:

P. Trilby PC 903/Start Time 7:00 a.m.
7:00 a.m. Scotland Yard Briefing 40 min.
7:40 a.m. Patrol Whitehall 15
7:55 a.m. Patrol Parliament Street 17
8:12 a.m. Patrol Broad Sanctuary 28
8:40 a.m. Patrol Victoria Street 17
8:57 a.m. Patrol Palace Road 9
9:06 a.m. Patrol Grosvenor Gardens 8
9:14 a.m. Patrol Grosvenor Place 6
9:20 a.m. Patrol Hyde Park Corner 10
9:30 a.m. Patrol Piccadilly 65
10:35 a.m. Patrol Berkeley Street 22
10:57 a.m. Patrol Berkeley Square 8
11:05 a.m. Patrol Bruton Street 8
11:13 a.m. Patrol Berkeley Square 13
11:26 a.m. Patrol Mount Street 24
11:50 a.m. Patrol Park Lane 20
12:10 p.m. Patrol Hyde Park Corner 20
12:30 p.m. Patrol Palace Gardens 35
1:05 p.m. Patrol Bird Cage Walk 28
1:33 p.m. Patrol Great George Street 46
2:19 p.m. Patrol Parliament Street 41
3:00 p.m. Scotland Yard Debrief

C. Martin PC 495/Start Time 6:00 a.m.
6:00 a.m. Scotland Yard Briefing 38 min.
6:38 a.m. Patrol Whitehall 35
7:13 a.m. Patrol Parliament Street 13
7:26 a.m. Patrol Bridge Street 21
7:47 a.m. Cross Westminster Bridge 18
8:05 a.m. Patrol Belvedere Road 25
8:30 a.m. Cross Charing Cross Bridge 20
8:50 a.m. Patrol Northumberland
   Avenue 10
9:00 a.m. Patrol Charing Cross 17
9:17 a.m. Patrol Whitehall 5
9:22 a.m. Patrol St. James Park 18
9:40 a.m. Patrol Buckingham Palace 20
10:00 a.m. Patrol Green Park 28
10:28 a.m. Patrol Piccadilly 22
10:50 a.m. Patrol Old Bond Street 15
11:05 a.m. Patrol Bruton Street 10
11:15 a.m. Patrol Old Bond Street 15
11:30 a.m. Patrol Piccadilly 19
11:49 a.m. Patrol Green Park 41
12:30 p.m. Patrol St. James Park 90
2:00 p.m. Scotland Yard Debrief

W. Khoji PC 720/Start Time 8:00 a.m.
8:00 a.m. Scotland Yard Briefing 30 min.
8:30 a.m. Patrol Whitehall 18
8:48 a.m. Patrol St. James Park 17
9:05 a.m. Patrol Buckingham Palace 19
9:24 a.m. Patrol Constitution Hill 28
9:52 a.m. Patrol Green Park 26
10:18 a.m. Patrol Piccadilly 10
10:28 a.m. Patrol Old Bond Street 17
10:45 a.m. Patrol Bruton Street 5
10:50 a.m. Patrol Berkeley Square 6
10:56 a.m. Patrol Hill Street 8
11:04 a.m. Patrol Union Street 25
11:29 a.m. Patrol South Audley Street 43
12:12 p.m. Patrol Mount Street 63
1:15 p.m. Patrol Park Lane 20
1:35 p.m. Patrol Hyde Park Corner 7
1:42 p.m. Patrol Grosvenor Place 21
2:03 p.m. Patrol Grosvenor Gardens 12
2:15 p.m. Patrol Victoria Street 71
3:26 p.m. Patrol Broad Sanctuary 22
3:48 p.m. Patrol Parliament Street 12
4:00 p.m. Scotland Yard Debrief

Bruton Street was the key. Martin and Trilby both arrived there at the same time—11:05 a.m—and Khoji had just been there, from 10:45 a.m. to 10:50 a.m. Therefore, I knew that the murder must have taken place there—or at the least the body was left there—between 10:50 a.m. and 11:05 a.m.

Harry Pratt was working at the National Gallery at that time. Although it is nearby, he would surely have been missed by his superiors. He must not have been involved in McAvoy's murder.

WHO WAS WANTED?

Plotting the locations of the Knife's crimes on the map of London, I drew an X as instructed. It was obvious where he worked: the Horse Guards.

The Knife must therefore be the alias of Lloyd Hardiman. Because he was arrested on June 16, 1894—and is thankfully still safely in his cell—he

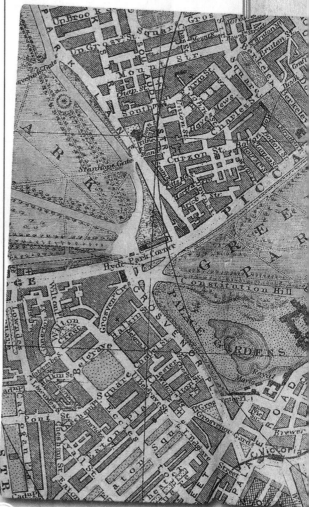

must have been in jail on June 18 when the murder was committed. This crime could not have been his.

DETAILS OF THE CRIME

The Detailed Crime Report describes five crimes: horse theft, fraud, evading arrest, attempted murder, and vandalization. Jamison Yttri

has committed four of these in the past, so this crime report must be describing him. He was arrested on June 15 and is expected to be in jail "for some time," meaning that he would not have been able to be present at the scene of the murder. He, therefore, is innocent of this murder, at least.

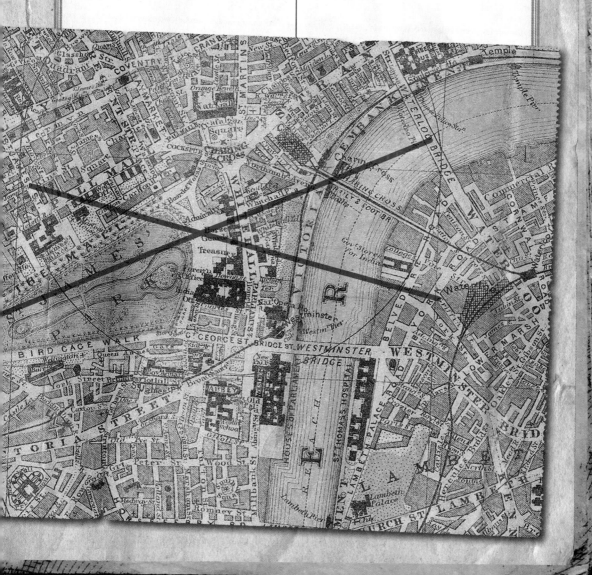

The Vandal of Connaught Road

Of the two remaining suspects, only one had a regular place of work: Duncan Greaves, the store assistant with a history of vandalization. But that left only one remaining suspect that could have committed the murder . . .

Holmes?

Cell Number Five

When we entered the evidence room, Lestrade had been called away to remove Greaves from his cell—road-sign vandalism is not a particularly grievous crime, after all—and we had overheard that the rest of the cells were full.

It was clear to Holmes that we would have to be held together in Greaves's old cell.

The Cells

Roll the Die

Starting at the bottom left square and first rolling upward, I followed the following sequence:

The grid spells: Start-Eros-Harvey-Bars-Candles-X:KDDKDDDKDDD DKFFDDDKKDDFDDDKDDKD.

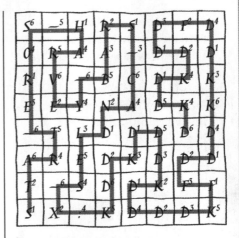

Eros

I took the string of letters over to the cogs and turned the crank (with some difficulty) until the "IN" arrow pointed first at K, then D, then F. The large output cog spun around, too, and the "OUT" arrow pointed to V, then I, then X, respectively. Therefore, I was left with a new string of letters:
VIIVIIIVIIIIVXXIIIVVIIXIIIVIIVI

Harvey

The grid's next clue took me to the shard of mirror, thanks to the name imprinted upon it. Examining it closely, there were no other markings and briefly I was stumped. Suddenly, I recognized that I was thinking too literally—the mirror was a symbol of what to do next with the sequence of letters: mirror it.

I was left with:
IVIIVIIIXIIVVIIIXXVIIIIVIIIVIIV

The Painted Bars

I knew that my mirror reversal was the correct move when I noticed that the four letters marked on the wall matched the first four letters of my sequence: I V II. What's more, I now understood what I should have done as soon as I saw the letters produced by the cogs—they were Roman numerals.

Now, I just had to understand the meaning of the white paint. After no small amount of time spent staring at the bars, I realized that the paint could be imagined as a series of horizontal lines drawn across the bars themselves. Where the paint carried on straight across the bar, so would the lines. Where the paint stopped halfway across the bar, it meant that the line started (if the paint ran from the center of the bar to the right) or stopped (if the paint ran from the center of the bar to the left) there.

Using the information I could glean from the numerals that were already marked on the wall, I presumed that the presence of the lines—and, importantly, the gaps between them—told me how to place and split the numerals in the sequence I already had. Thus, I could split the letters as follows: I V II VIII XII V VIII XX VI III VIII VII V.

This provided me with the numbers: 1 5 2 8 12 5 8 20 6 3 8 7 5

Happy Birthday

I blew out the candles swiftly, hoping we were not too late to solve this puzzle. Fortunately, it appears this shadowy organization had access to high-quality wax. I measured the heights of the candles against the markings on the ruler, and scribbled the following pattern in my notebook:

△ ∿ ∿ ⊖ ☆ ⊖ ∿ △ △ ∿ ⊖ ☆ ☆

The Graffitied Wall

The symbols on the ruler were the same as on the strange design on the wall. Now that I knew what they were, it seemed obvious to me that they were telling me directions, as clearly as the points on a compass.

After I realized that both of my sequences were thirteen entries long, I combined them, so I now had: 1 Up, 5 Right, 2 Right, 8 Down, 12 Left, 5 Down, 8 Right, 20 Up, 6 Up, 3 Right, 8 Down, 7 Left, 5 Left.

Starting on the red brick marked X, I followed the instructions, landing on the letters as I went. The message was stark: HIDDENINBIBLE. Hidden in the Bible!

The Circus

Xellda's Enigmas

Xellda had said that this was the only order that counted, so I thought that I had better begin with her riddles. They took some unraveling, but without too much delay I had the answers:

Death cannot be delayed or cheated, and everyone meets it in the end.

Justice has scales that bring satisfaction against wrong-doers.

Strength can be of both conviction and physical muscles.

The world is all around us, and where we all lie.

Importantly, I realized where I had seen each of these answers before.

The Prophetic Cyphstress

I thought back to the tarot cards that the Cyphstress had shown us. Each of the riddles' answers were represented by those cards. But what could that mean? I had no mystic ability myself to call upon that might help me interpret them.

However, I did remember something unusual about the tarot cards. Each had a symbol drawn upon it that I was certain was not a normal feature of a deck. These four symbols might have some other meaning. I would, however, have to look elsewhere to discover it.

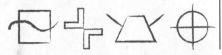

The Bewilder Box

It was no small feat of engineering, but I managed to fit the squares together to create a satisfactory cube. Walking around it, I noticed that the designs in each of the eight corners—when viewed from the correct angle—appeared to create letters. What was more, each of those letters was next to one of the tarot symbols.

The four symbols that I had previously marked out as significant were next to the C (Death), the T (Justice), the H (Strength), and the Y (The World).

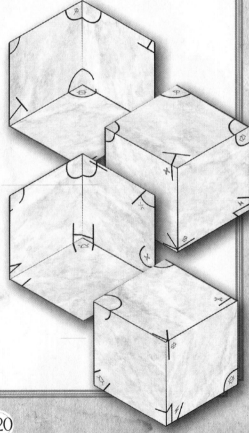

THE STAR ATTRACTIONS

The figures in each of the four posters were in unusual positions. Although, perhaps not so unusual for circus antics, but, nevertheless, the fact remained that they directly matched positions from the Dancing Man cipher that Holmes had solved.

The Ringmaster was a Y, the Clown was a T, the Strongman was a C, and the Juggler an H. The very same four letters that I had just discovered. Placing them in the same order as Xellda's riddles, which she had made clear was important, meant the correct sequence was the Strongman followed by the Clown, the Juggler, and the Ringmaster.

However, I felt like I was missing something. Those artists did not appear anywhere else around the circus, as far as I could see. Something else tugged at my attention, but I could not yet place my finger on what it was.

BALL TOSS

As soon as I realized that the tube and ball colors matched the poster background colors, I knew that I was on the right track. The important sequence was not the circus artists, but the colors that they represented: purple, red, blue, black.

Next, I gathered the balls scattered around the circus. It did not seem necessary for me to try my hand at the game itself—and potentially embarrass myself in front of Holmes. The funnels were probably intentionally designed to bounce the balls out, anyway. Instead, I simply counted them. There were four purple balls, three red, six blue (including the one in the tube), and five black.

A TICKET TO THE FINALE

I rushed back to the tickets and flipped through them as fast as I could. I had a hunch, and, sure enough, it was proved correct. The balls had given me four numbers in a specific order: 4-3-6-5. One of the tickets was marked with that exact same sequence of numbers. I knew where we had to go next.

The Royal Strand Theater.

THE THEATER

COSTUME CONUNDRUM

The set list helped me to identify three costumes immediately. The assistant must wear a red dress, and, in the introduction, Harry Houdini wears a smart suit, while he wears a similar suit but with inverted colors for the finale. This must mean the black suit and the white suit with the top hats.

The descriptions of the two acts are unhelpful, but the posters in the lobby told me that their titles were "Victoria and the Butler" and the

aforementioned "Detective's End."
On the rack was a policeman's outfit,
which I had to assume would fit the
bill for "Detective's End," and what
looked like a butler's outfit right next
to a regal dress.

That left only one costume, and it
was one that I thought I recognized:
the train ticket collector's uniform.

I had seen it only yesterday.

MATCHING CURTAINS

I recognized the knot designs on the
curtains to be the same as the knots
hanging from the labeled ropes. I
could, therefore, associate each knot
on the curtain with a letter. From top
to bottom they were: G, A, D, F, H,
B, E, C.

I pulled the two halves of the
curtains together, which meant that
the "ropes" now ran in unbroken
paths across both halves, from the
knots to the animals. Following the
paths, I found: G–Shark, A–Rabbit,
D–Giraffe, F–Elephant, H–Rooster,
B–Rhino, E–Cat, C–Camel.

A BUMPY TIME

I quickly asked Sherlock to repeat
his description. Comparing it with
my ruler, it was clear that the first set
of six described a C, with the black
pins standing in for where the bumps
would be. The second set was an F,
and the third was an H.

HANGING PROPS

The three important letters were C, F,
and H. That much I had established.
The animals associated with those
letters were the camel, the elephant, and
the rooster. So far, so good. But what to
do with that information?

Glancing over at Holmes, it was
clear that time was running out. The
water was almost up to his shoulders.
As much as I tried, I could not glean
anything meaningful from the braille
alphabet. That was not the correct path
to explore, it would seem.

I was just beginning to despair when
I was struck by a flash of inspiration.
Perhaps it was the pattern not of each
of the three animals individually, but
of each of the three animals combined,
that I should be experimenting with.

I imagined the three boards stacked
on top of each other, and an obvious
series of shapes appeared before my
eyes.

3, 2, 1! That was the code. It was
time to free Holmes.

Image shown on page 224.

THE FINAL ESCAPE

I still had the long, thin, and all-
important *hollow* metal tube in my
hand. I brought one end to my lips and
slid the other through the grate to create
my own improvised snorkel. I took a
deep breath of beautiful fresh air and
had never felt so relieved in all my life!

BONUS PUZZLE
The boy was Stanley Spencer, an artist famed for his paintings depicting biblical scenes occurring as if in Cookham. It appears Holmes helped inspire his artistic talents.

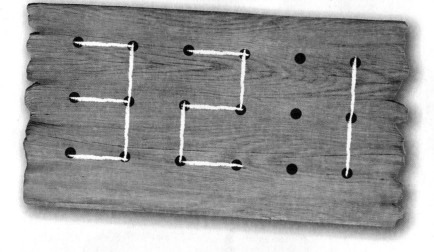

The publishers would like to thank the following sources for their kind permission to reproduce the pictures in this book.

All images and backgrounds are © Shutterstock except:

Page 11 (right): LordRunar/iStock; 27: Library of Congress Prints and Photographs; 28 (top): thislife pictures/Alamy Stock Photo; 28 (left): Library of Congress Prints and Photographs; 28 (right): thislife pictures/Alamy Stock Photo; 29 (top): Library of Congress Prints and Photographs; 29 (left): thislife pictures/Alamy Stock Photo; 29 (right): thislife pictures/Alamy Stock Photo.

Every effort has been made to acknowledge correctly and contact the source and/or copyright holder of each picture. Any unintentional errors or omissions will be corrected in future editions of this book.